The Controversy about Economic Growth

Edited by

Ben Turok

First published by Jacana Media (Pty) Ltd in 2011

10 Orange Street
Sunnyside
Auckland Park 2092
South Africa
+2711 628 3200
www.jacana.co.za

ISBN 978-1-77009-967-8

Set in Minion 10.5/14pt
Printed and bound by Ultra Litho (Pty) Limited, Johannesburg
Job No. 001414

See a complete list of Jacana titles at www.jacana.co.za

Contents

The Controversy about Economic Growth

Acknowledgements

Thanks are due to Aneesah Reynolds, who typed numerous complicated tapes; Helen Douglas, who edited the oral presentations and organised the text; Germaine Habiyaremye, who arranged the logistics of the seminar series; the Friedrich-Ebert-Stiftung (FES) in South Africa, which assisted with the funding of the seminars; Ravi Naidoo, Group Executive, Development Planning at the Development Bank of Southern Africa (DBSA), who coordinated DBSA's involvement in the seminar series; and Janine Thorne and Michele Ruiters, who edited the volume.

Contributors

Ben Turok is a Member of the South African Parliament and editor of *New Agenda: South African Journal of Social and Economic Policy*

Ben Cousins is the Department of Science and Technology/ National Research Foundation Chair in Poverty, Land and Agrarian Studies and Senior Professor, Institute for Poverty, Land and Agrarian Studies (PLAAS), University of the Western Cape

Jeremy Cronin is Deputy Minister of Transport and member of the South African Communist Party

Rob Davies is Minister of Trade and Industry

Charlotte du Toit is Chief Executive, Plus Economics, and Professor of Economics, University of Pretoria

Richard Goode is Infrastructure Specialist, Development Bank of Southern Africa; formerly Technical Specialist, Mineral Economics Division, Council for Mineral Technology (Mintek)

Jorge Maia is Head of Research and Information, Industrial Development Corporation

Neva Makgetla is Deputy Director-General, Economic Development Department; formerly the Lead Economist, Development Planning Division, Development Bank of Southern Africa and the Sector Strategies Coordinator in the Presidency

Seeraj Mohamed is Director, Corporate Strategy and Industrial Development Research Programme, School of Economic and Business Sciences, University of the Witwatersrand

Ravi Naidoo is Group Executive, Development Planning Division, Development Bank of Southern Africa

Nnzeni Netshitomboni is Senior Industry Analyst, Research and Information Centre, Industrial Development Corporation

Simon Roberts is Chief Economist, Competition Commission of South Africa

Nimrod Zalk is Deputy Director-General, Department of Trade and Industry

Abbreviations

ANC	African National Congress
AsgiSA	Accelerated and Shared Growth Initiative for South Africa
BBBEE	broad-based black economic empowerment
BEE	black economic empowerment
BNDES	Banco Nacional de Desenvolvimento Econômico e Social
CODESA	Convention for a Democratic South Africa
COSATU	Congress of South African Trade Unions
CSDP	Competitive Supplier Development Programme
DBSA	Development Bank of Southern Africa Ltd
the dti	Department of Trade and Industry
EPWP	Extended Public Works Programme
FAT	Workers' Assistance Fund
FES	Friedrich-Ebert-Stiftung
FIRE	finance, insurance and real estate
GDP	gross domestic product
GEAR	Growth, Employment and Redistribution
HIV/AIDS	Human Immunodeficiency Virus/Acquired Immune Deficiency Syndrome
ICT	information and communication technology
IDC	Industrial Development Corporation
ILO	International Labour Office
IPAP	Industrial Policy Action Plan
JSE	Johannesburg Stock Exchange

MIDP	Motor Industry Development Programme
NDR	National Democratic Revolution
NEHAWU	National Education, Health and Allied Workers' Union
NIPP	National Industrial Participation Programme
OTK	Oos-Transvaal Koöperasie
PIC	Public Investment Commission
PLAAS	Institute for Poverty, Land and Agrarian Studies
RDP	Reconstruction and Development Programme
REFIT	renewable energy feed-in tariff
SADTU	South African Democratic Teachers Union
SAFCOL	South African Forestry Company Ltd
SAFEX	South African Futures Exchange
SANAS	South African National Accreditation System
SETA	Sector Education and Training Authority
SMME	small, medium and microenterprise
TJLP	long-term interest rate (Brazil)
UDF	United Democratic Front

Preface

From November 2009 to May 2010, the Development Bank of Southern Africa (DBSA) co-hosted an economic seminar series with *New Agenda: South African Journal of Social and Economic Policy* and the Friedrich Ebert Foundation. The series, entitled 'Prospects for Economic Transformation', was convened to understand the economy and the potential for the state and social partners to transform it.

The five seminars covered the following topics: the structure of the economy, the value chain, potential resources for development, 'Is a Great Leap possible?', and, finally, building sufficient consensus for what was termed a developmental growth path.

The discussions ultimately focused on the 'economic structure', those long-term tendencies that reflect the core economic institutions which produce the development outcomes we see today. These tendencies – such as ownership, the spatial pattern of production, allocation of education and skills – remain stubbornly in place throughout business cycles and change only slowly over time. Yet the pressure to eradicate pervasive and persistent unemployment and poverty remains an urgent, and indeed growing, challenge to South Africa's future. What is to be done? Equally important, who will do it and how should it be done? The South African experience post-1994 is a sober reminder that at the same time as we muddle through a complex and contested implementation, a new vision has to be renegotiated. The scope of discussions in the seminar series was thus alive to the need to blend in aspects of a vision alongside hard-nosed lessons of implementation.

To facilitate dissemination of this important debate, these seminars have been incorporated as a co-publication in this Jacana series. The book is the product of a non-partisan exercise bringing together decision-makers and leading analysts who work within the contested terrain that is the state. The analysis is relevant for all stakeholders and political parties.

We hope that the book will stimulate open and frank discussion on the structural constraints facing a developmental growth path for South Africa. Moreover, we hope that this book stimulates new and effective approaches to overcoming these constraints.

Ravi Naidoo

Introduction

Ben Turok

Many documents acknowledge that South Africa inherited a particular accumulation model that has not changed. The Green Paper on Planning, for example, says that the structure of the economy has not changed for a hundred years. This must be a concern for everyone. If the structure has not changed, then what has changed? Clearly, there has been a change in the social provision of various services, but we are left with *structural* poverty, unemployment and inequality. Haroon Bhorat recently briefed Parliament that South Africa is now the most unequal society in the world. This was quite a shock, even though we knew that inequality is the same now as it was in 1994.

South African economic policy under democracy (Aron et al, 2009) shows that the economic policies of the government have merely been adjustments. The state's agenda for inclusive growth does not reflect the need for structural change. Indeed, it gives a sense of trying to include people through adjustments.

Rather than reforms that are conceived as adjustments for amelioration here and there, this book attempts to envisage reforms that will create a platform for a fundamental structural advance. South Africa desperately needs a vision of fundamental change.

The series of five seminars on which this book is based was held in the context of ever-increasing concern about the scale of inequality, unemployment and poverty in South Africa. These social problems are directly related to the inherited structure of the economy; the recession has only worsened the underlying problems. This seminar series attempted to open the door to a vision of reforms leading to structural change. It started from the premise that attempts at amelioration and reform will not work without structural change and tried to determine what can be done now to create a platform for the next 10, 20 or 30 years.

Reference

Aron, J, Kahn, B & Kingdon, G (eds), 2009. *South African economic policy under democracy.* Oxford and New York: Oxford University Press.

Part One

The Structure of the Economy

Opening remarks

Ben Turok

Developing a framework for analysis

The discussion centred on the importance of reviving class analysis in understanding the South African economy and the potential for strong policy interventions in the economy.

The focus on class arose from the question of what is meant by *economic structure*. The term typically refers to long-term tendencies that reflect the core institutions of the economy. These tendencies remain in place throughout business cycles and change only slowly over time. Elements of the economic structure include ownership, production, the spatial structure of settlements and production, and the distribution of education and skills.

The issue of structural problems arises in South Africa mainly because extraordinarily high levels of joblessness and inequality persist 15 years after the transition to democracy. The International Labour Office (ILO) ranks South Africa as one of ten countries with unusually low levels of employment: fewer than half of all working-age adults in the country have income-earning employment, as against a worldwide norm of almost two thirds.

The structural factors behind the high joblessness in South Africa were shaped under the apartheid regime. Africans were systematically marginalised, both spatially – by forcing them to live far from economic centres – and institutionally, by depriving them of resources, formal qualifications and access to financial and other market institutions. During this time, the mining value chain became central to the economy while the manufacturing and services sectors remained relatively underdeveloped.

A more recent development, especially since the late 1990s, has been a growing dependence on short-term capital inflows during periods of excess liquidity in the international economy. This has been mirrored in a reduced dependence on domestic resources to finance investment. It is important to understand how these trends affected and reflected changes in the nature of South African capital, especially in mining, manufacturing and financial interests.

The emphasis on structural issues, including class, contrasts with explanations of joblessness that focus exclusively on factors that raise the cost of business overall, such as wages, infrastructure, skill shortages, taxes or government borrowing. A structural explanation can accommodate the analyses of these particular constraints but also goes beyond them.

Capital

A class analysis of the South African economy should explore the development of both capital and labour. By definition, there is a dialectical relationship between capital relations (in the sense of who owns and controls economic activity) and the production structure. This relationship both reflects and shapes decisions on resource use in the economy.

The distribution of ownership in the South African economy is even more inequitable than the distribution of income. There is almost no data for tracking ownership but it is typically highly concentrated in mining economies. The apartheid system also left South Africa with a tiny small and micro sector in comparison to other middle-income countries, while the upstream manufacturing, finance, retail and telecommunications sectors are highly concentrated. This concentration has allowed monopoly pricing on wage goods and vital inputs, which makes the economy less efficient and raises the cost of employment.

It is important to track the development of capital, which has undergone substantial changes since the transition to democracy. Specifically, an analysis is needed of the evolving aims and power of the following groups:

- The minerals-energy complex
- Other domestic private capital groups, such as black economic empowerment (BEE) groups, 'new' sectors and agriculture
- State capital, in state-owned enterprises, development finance institutions and others.

In the past 15 years, South Africa has experienced a massive expansion in financial capital, although without the extremes of speculative behaviour seen in the global North. The privatisation of services has led to rapid growth in other forms of capital, notably in health, security services and telecommunications. Capital growth was rapid largely because the market dominance of monopolies and oligopolies in these industries was left in place during the commercialisation. This has resulted in higher costs, especially for skilled employment. A particular problem for the economy is the high cost of telecommunications and financial services. However, since these sectors have also proved important for narrow forms of BEE, regulating them is politically difficult. Another shift has been the decline in domestic mining capital, much of which has been reintegrated into international capital groups. In this process, the conglomerate structure has been fragmented and the centres of control have moved overseas. The restructuring of capital is reflected in the changing positions of different sectors on the Johannesburg Stock Exchange (JSE): for example, health, retail and telecommunications moved up the rankings.

Given the concentration of ownership, its racial composition has been very slow to change. This has led to pressure on the state from emerging black capital. In effect, state-owned enterprises and parts of the public service have functioned as a path into business for black entrepreneurs. The result has been conflicting mandates, as the state tried to balance the demands for BEE, better service delivery and commercial sustainability. There is clearly a need for a systematic analysis of the impact of this process on development.

State capital includes the development finance institutions and the Public Investment Commission (PIC). These institutions should play an important role in changing the structure of production. While the PIC owns shares in major South African companies (e.g. 10% of Old Mutual), it does not have a developmental agenda for them. Instead, it has focused on supporting narrow BEE. State agencies have also begun to compete for funds from the PIC or the Government Employees Pension Fund; this is a risky process, which must be managed strategically.

It is important to analyse how the short-term inflows into the JSE and bonds affect (a) real investment and domestic savings, and (b) the structure of capital. Another topic to explore is how the state can use measures to channel investment, infrastructure, education and skills development in ways that support a more equitable and dynamic structure of capital and production.

Economic diversification

The minerals value chain (which includes the production of the base metals and heavy chemicals that statistically count as manufacturing) contributes around 10% of employment and the gross domestic product (GDP). However, it accounts for well over half of South Africa's exports. This reflects the dominance of the minerals-energy complex, which is rooted in the state's production of electricity from coal.

This leads to a number of strategic issues.

- Since prices were relatively low for much of the 1990s, the state initially ignored mining because of the perception that it was a declining industry. This perception was reversed during the commodity boom of the mid-2000s. What is seen as the future driver of the economy?
- Since mining will remain important in the near future, the government needs to determine how it can maximise export revenues while enabling more equitable access to rents. A particular weakness has been the tendency to focus on narrow BEE without ensuring that the sector has the infrastructure and skills it needs for sustainable growth.
- The ability of the state to support job creation by diversifying the economy changes over time. In the very short run, only direct subsidies or employment by the state can create jobs. In the medium term, the government must support labour-absorbing industries that create and upgrade employment on a mass scale. It must also lay the basis for long-term growth by continuing its support for knowledge-intensive industries. There is, however, a trade-off because all of these activities call for substantial state resources.
- The capacity of the state to affect the structure of production is limited. Specific obstacles are:
  (a) The lack of a well-considered and systematic methodology for identifying sectors that can create mass employment and for addressing the constraints to their growth
  (b) The institutional blockages that prevent the provision of infrastructure and skills in support of new economic activities
  (c) The lack of policy coherence across the state, which may lead to contradictory priorities and regulatory burdens that are excessively costly

(d) The absence of systems to channel resources from the private sector into developmental programmes.

- How far can South Africa go in holding down the value of the currency, and which industries will be viable if the currency stays moderately strong? Financial 'speed bumps' are certainly a critical step towards addressing South Africa's slow recovery from the international financial crisis.
- There is a regional question: should people move to urban centres or should the state try to overcome service and investment backlogs in the former Bantustans?
- Whatever the economic structure, the state has to ensure adequate economic infrastructure, education and training. However, inevitable choices in that context also shape the production structure and social mobility.

1. Essence of the inherited structure

Neva Makgetla

This presentation defines the economic structure, examines a range of structural weaknesses and then briefly addresses some implications.

What is meant by 'economic structure'?

The economic structure includes ownership, the structure of production and the structure of exports. There is also the spatial structure, the financial system, and education and skills. All of these have one thing in common: they continue right through business cycles. Structural concerns remain a problem whether the economy is growing or contracting. It is, therefore, important to change the basic social and economic institutions in order to change the outcomes they generate.

It may be asked whether economic growth for, say, five years will effect a structural change. This is unlikely – the longer-term trends do not change even when the economy is growing. In South Africa, the primary longer-term trends are the extremely low levels of employment and high inequalities.

Structuralist vs other approaches

A *structural* explanation of these trends incorporates two central factors. First, it points to apartheid and the way it marginalised people, particularly Africans. This marginalisation was both spatial, by pushing them out of the economic centres, and institutional, by excluding them from the core market institutions. Second, it highlights the central role of the minerals value chain, which contributed to the relative underdevelopment of manufacturing and many services. In effect, a structural analysis asks what it means to be a resource-based economy and, specifically, one that is built on a racially exclusive system.

A more recent structural concern is that South Africa tends to depend on short-term capital inflows rather than generating its own savings to fund investment. In the long run, this pattern chokes off growth.

A structural explanation for poverty and inequality is fundamentally different from explanations based on factors such as the cost of business, wages, infrastructure, core skills shortages, or taxes and government borrowing. Such non-structuralist analyses can come from either the liberal left or the right.

What sets the structural approach apart is this question: does a country focus on getting the crosscutting 'fundamentals' right or does it target particular interventions that will openly benefit some groups rather than others? A few years ago, a World Bank report on competitiveness and development explicitly said that a country should use only crosscutting measures because targeted measures distort markets. So, much of the debate is about how a country sees markets. The structural approach usually requires the state to favour some groups over others. That, in itself, is a political choice.

Growth, employment and remuneration

Looking at the numbers behind the structural concerns, South Africa has grown at almost exactly the average rate for the world economy, and close to the growth rate of other middle-income countries (see Figure 1.1). Only low-income countries such as China, India and other parts of Asia have achieved much higher growth rates, as have low-income countries in Africa.

Figure 1.1: Growth rates, 1994 to 2009

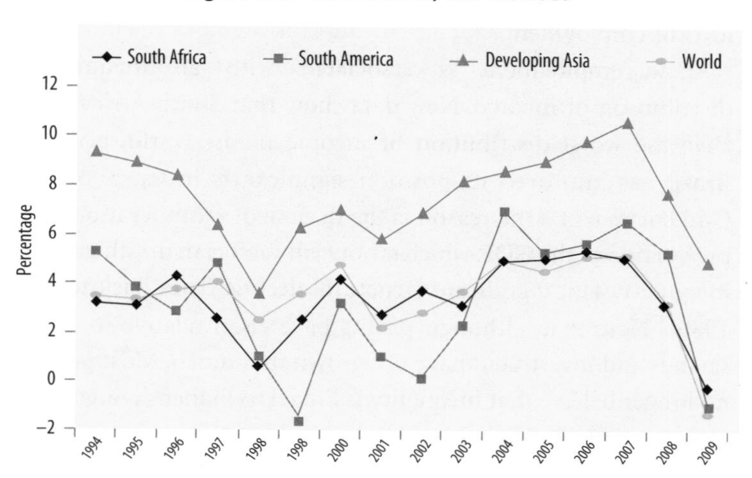

It is probably unrealistic to hope that South Africa can simply grow out of its troubles by achieving the levels of growth of China and India. South Africa can do well; indeed, it can do much better than it has done so far. However, it is not realistic to expect 6% growth for extended periods, despite what the models may say. No other middle-income country has managed such growth for long.

Associated with this is the particularly low rate of employment in the country. Less than 50% of the working-age population has income-generating employment, including self-employment, in the more developed parts of the country. In the former Bantustans, the proportion is less than 30%, as against an observed statistic of 64%.

A recent ILO paper puts South Africa among the ten countries with the worst employment ratios. It is also one of only five where gender difference is not the main cause. Many Arabic countries have low employment ratios because women do not work. However, South Africa ranks with countries such as Macedonia that do not have a big difference in the participation rates of men and women but still have an extraordinarily low level of employment.

Low employment is associated with an inequitable distribution of income. New data show that South Africa may have the worst distribution of income in the world, because Brazil has improved its position significantly in terms of the Gini coefficient. One reason is the decline of remuneration as a proportion of the GDP, which is normally associated with greater inequality. This significant structural decline dates back to the 1980s. Note that, although profits have risen relative to GDP, savings and investment have not grown that much. Most people no longer believe that inequality is linked to higher savings and, thus, to growth. High inequalities tend to undermine savings rather than support it. The decline in remuneration relative to the GDP is why the Congress of South African Trade Unions (COSATU) argued that business benefited more from liberation than labour. Of course, the remuneration data also include a few executives who earn R5 million a year. So, it is not a direct class picture but it is the closest available.

There is a problem of perception: people at the top compare themselves with executives in Europe and the United States but they want to pay ordinary workers like they were in China or India. It is often argued that this is because of the skills shortage but it still leads to a growing wage gap. In the North, the pay for top people in business has risen more rapidly than overall incomes. South Africa does not have similar pay packages for top executives; they are a different order of magnitude. But the wage gap still means that South Africa does not have the kind of social solidarity that will overcome income inequalities and create a more cohesive society. Income inequality puts significant pressure on policy. It makes it hard to create a consistent development or growth policy because the people at the bottom will not take a long-term perspective as long as those at the top live in luxury. The countries that managed to develop had a kind of social pact where, even if people at the top earned a lot, they at least did not consume it conspicuously. The situation in South Africa is not as bad as in the United States but it might be sufficiently bad that building a coalition for change would be impossible.

Another factor is the spatial structure: the average income is about three times higher in metropolitan areas than it is in the former Bantustan regions. In every case, because of the inequalities, the median is significantly less than the average.

Structures of ownership

The distribution of ownership is generally more inequitable than the distribution of income, but there is very little data on the precise structure of ownership in South Africa. Mining economies tend to be highly concentrated because of the economies of scale in mining and the way it is financed. In South Africa, the highest levels of concentration tend to be in the upstream industries and in retail and telecommunications. These affect the rest of the economy through monopoly pricing on wage goods and vital inputs. There is also evidence that monopolised retail sectors tend to foster concentration and higher prices in the supply industries (i.e. manufacturing and agriculture). In addition, monopoly pricing makes the inputs used by industry more expensive.

The concentration of private capital has also been associated with very slow change in its racial composition. Big business is still predominantly white and that, in turn, puts pressure on the state to focus on creating opportunities for black capital rather than on broader transformation. This has significant political implications, in addition to the immediate economic issues.

State capital is embodied in major state-owned enterprises, such as Denel, Transnet and Eskom. While they have a large impact on economic development, they face conflicting mandates. For one, there is a narrow BEE practice of bringing black management and owners into these enterprises just because private capital is resistant to doing so. Then there is the pressure to provide services to households and core infrastructure for the economy. It is not clear how this conflict can be managed without a clear mandate for the role of state-owned enterprises.

Finally, the small and micro sector in South Africa is limited compared to that of other middle-income countries. With apartheid having excluded people for so many years, the country has neither the institutions nor the traditions to support small firms. The advanced manufacturing and concentrated retail sectors effectively keep out competition, in part by offering better and cheaper goods and services than small firms can provide.

Sectoral composition

Mining is critical to the South African economy. While it contributes only about 10% of the GDP, 10% of employment and 20% of investment, if base metals and heavy chemicals are included then mining contributes over half of total exports. The last decade has seen a significant shift in the structure of mining exports: gold exports have declined while platinum has increased. Since gold is more countercyclical and much more labour-intensive than platinum, the declining share of gold exports has resulted in a smaller stabilisation effect and significant job losses.

The rest of the world sees South Africa as a mining-based economy, despite claims that manufacturing exports had grown. Most of this increase in manufactured exports was from base metals, which, once refined, count as manufacturing. But exporting steel does not make the country a high-level manufacturer. Where manufactured exports *have* grown is in cars, which accounted for about 7% of exports before the crisis. (However, this sector is highly subsidised.)

The sectoral composition of the GDP shows that mining has increased overall. It first declined in the 1990s when commodity prices were low, then increased as commodity prices rose from 2008 and is likely to have declined again since. The share of manufacturing has declined, even including base metals. The services sector has generally grown, especially business and financial services. Note that this sector includes information technology, information services, security services and real estate. In employment terms, financial services account for a relatively small share of employment in the services sector.

Prospects for employment

What are the implications for employment and, hence, for inclusion? When the GDP grew, there was relatively rapid growth in employment, mainly in the tertiary industries. Growth was driven by the increase in global commodity prices and the related capital inflows, which resulted in a lower interest rate, more consumer power and higher investment.

However, the bulk of the job creation was not in mining or manufacturing; it was mainly in the services, construction and retail sectors. There was a decline in agricultural employment, although employment in this sector is seasonal, tends to react sharply and is badly measured. This pattern of job creation in the labour-intensive sectors, mainly services, is evident worldwide. It implies that employment is being created through a multiplier effect, which may not be desirable. A more systematic approach to this issue is clearly needed.

The majority of workers in the formal retail sector are paid R2 500 to R3 000 a month (2008 figures). While wages are low, neither this nor construction is the lowest-paid sector. The lowest wages are in the domestic, informal and agriculture sectors; here, half of the workers earn less than R1 000 per month, on average. Services do tend to be highly dichotomised. The economy has large top, middle and bottom levels of skilled people, and then it has elementary workers, like security and domestic workers, who are particularly poorly paid.

There is also a spatial issue. Gauteng, which accounts for 20% of the population, has about 35% of total employment. Much of this is in the advanced industries, where Gauteng is far more dominant than the other metropolitan areas. The province accounts for more than half of employment in business and financial services and close to 40% of employment in manufacturing.

Capital flows

A final issue is the structural problem of capital flows. With the growth in recent years, South Africa went into a deficit on the balance of trade. There was a higher outflow of both services and income payments relative to the GDP. This was associated with high capital inflows, mainly into bonds and equity. Foreign investment accounted for up to 80% of all new investment funds, while there was a rapid decline in real private savings for much of the growth period.

The argument around this issue can be constructed as follows: South Africa does not borrow but it is still dependent on short-term capital inflows. Although the debt service ratio seems sound, the country is just as dependent on short-term capital inflows as other middle-income countries. It pays for this not just in the form of interest payments but also in dividends. Private company savings equals company profits less dividends. The outflow of dividends meant that private company savings plummeted. But capital inflows also raise the value of the rand and help to moderate inflation. As a result, interest rates declined and the households that could borrow (i.e. the upper 20%) expanded their debt, mostly for cars and housing. The country soon had its own miniature housing bubble and household savings became negative.

Clearly, the dependence on short-term capital inflows has a number of negative effects that are not well managed, in part because the debt service ratio seems lower than in other middle-income countries. However, the heavy dependence on short-term capital outflows does bring vulnerabilities, including a volatile currency. There is a direct correlation between a declining stock market and the value of the rand.

Job losses

There has been a rapid acceleration of job losses in the formal sector in the last three months, and other sectors are doing even worse. The numbers are worrying. From the last quarter of 2008 to July 2009, 2% of formal jobs were lost. In the last three months of 2009, another 3% were lost. The country has now lost 5% of all formal jobs and between 12% and 15% of jobs in the rest of the economy.

It is not clear whether this is a structural or episodic phenomenon but it does point to the problem with such a multiplier effect: it also works backwards. When the core economy shrinks, the periphery may lose even more jobs, hurting those who are relatively unskilled and already extremely poor.

On a sectoral level, manufacturing saw enormous job losses for the first time in 2009. The state sector has been crucial for stability because it lost relatively few jobs. The retail and construction sectors also saw fewer than expected losses. Construction job losses are mostly in housing and have been offset by the infrastructure programme; the stimulus programme is clearly still working. In the mining and manufacturing sectors, however, employers seem to have resisted retrenchment as long as they could and then gave in, all at once, in the last three months.

A particular social problem – which is probably a structural issue – is that the highest rates of unemployment are among the youth, and so are the biggest job losses. People aged 15 to 24 lost one out of seven jobs (about 14%) in 2009, whereas older people have lost 5% or 6%.

Areas of concern

The election manifesto of the African National Congress (ANC) held that the creation of decent work opportunities has to be the main criterion for economic policy. In line with this manifesto and the Polokwane Resolutions, a phased approach is clearly needed.

Mining

Mining is not about to disappear. As the main source of exports, mining is critical to growth across the economy. South Africa faces resource dependence, the so-called 'resource curse', because the government does not really have a strategy to maximise the benefits and minimise the costs of mining. It is not clear what the country wants from mining. How can it ensure that mining exports are maximised over the medium to long run, or as long as they are needed?

There are three concerns. First, pursuing narrow BEE is very expensive and will harm the mining industry unless it gets the infrastructure and inputs it needs to sustain output. Second, the country is exporting its rich minerals without beneficiation, timing or planning how to maximise output in the medium to long term; it is running through its resources much too fast. It is not clear that the government has a strategy on either issue. Also, how can the government ensure that the mining rents, which have been crucial for South Africa's development, are used to benefit the majority in the long run?

Structural change is sometimes seen as focusing on the new and ignoring the old. However, the country cannot just walk away from the old: mining will remain important for a long time. It has to be made to work in the transition period.

Employment creation

The creation of employment in the short term, whether in response to an immediate or a long-term crisis, is possible only through state subsidies or employment schemes such as the

Extended Public Works Programme (EPWP) Phase 2. But are these programmes being rolled out fast enough to deal with the current crisis? Are they on the right scale?

In the medium term, as the Medium-Term Budget Policy Statement asked, is policy sufficiently focused on sectors that can create employment? What about the sectors that do not have the best working conditions but can create employment rapidly because the cost per job is lower? What would it mean to support jobs in the services, manufacturing, construction or retail sectors? How can decent work opportunities be ensured when the state does not have the capacity to support those sectors? At the same time, the high-tech industries that have previously attracted support cannot be written off. Given limited state capacity and resources, maintaining this balance is always a struggle, as the Industrial Policy Action Plan (IPAP) shows.

Monetary policy

Development in Asia depended in part on a stable and ongoing depreciation of local currencies. Given the level of international liquidity, is it possible for South Africa to depreciate its currency in this way? It is generally agreed that the value of the currency must be held down but how can this be achieved? Abolishing exchange controls is *not* the right way because it diminishes the country's ability to control its capital. Rather than encouraging capital outflows, the possibility of controlling capital inflows should be explored.

If the currency cannot depreciate, how does that affect which industries are viable and which are not? For the last ten years, South Africa has not managed the currency but tried to subsidise industries that were uncompetitive at that currency value. It could never provide sufficient subsidies to make these industries grow. What about industries that actually are competitive internationally at a high currency level, like agriculture and some of the services? What about the regional and domestic markets where industries are competitive even if the currency is relatively high? This is a fundamental policy question.

Regional investment

What are the regional and spatial implications of economic policy? South Africa is not homogeneous. Continuing on a standard economic path will create jobs mostly in the existing economic centres and depopulate the rest of the country. This has huge implications for government services, if nothing else (e.g. where to provide basic services and housing). Meanwhile, the Department of Trade and Industry (the dti) wants to create regional incentives to keep economic investment in areas that are otherwise not viable in terms of their infrastructure, location and skills. The Department of Rural Development and Land Reform is working on this but it affects all the economic departments, as well as the Department of Cooperative Governance and Traditional Affairs.

A final issue is crosscutting effects, particularly of economic infrastructure, education and training. When the state provides cheap electricity to the mines, it reinforces the dominance of mining in the economy while reducing the supply of electricity to agriculture, towns and cities. The resulting blackouts across the cities, in turn, affect the input sectors for the mines. Similarly, when proper transport is created, where and how it is done will affect the viability of some industries. The government has planned and rolled out infrastructure or education and training programmes as if the economy were not going to change, thereby reinforcing the existing structures rather than modifying them.

Discussion

Opening the discussion, Ben Turok emphasised that the purpose of the seminar series was to identify issues that would lead to structural change in the economy. Neva Makgetla began by asking for a shared working understanding of the

> *meaning of 'structural' in this context. The participants settled on three components: production and distribution; ownership and control; and the spatial structure.*

Concerning ownership, a broader definition is required, one that goes beyond shares to include land and housing as productive assets. One factor that has limited the accumulation of capital by BEE interests is the cost of capital versus its returns. Unless this is addressed, ownership will not be expanded in a meaningful way. Also, significant sums of state capital are embedded in state-owned enterprises like the PIC, where it is passive. A developmental state needs to have an influence over the financial sector. The PIC could play that role as a significant shareholder. (As for the Government Employees Pension Fund, this is an almost fully funded pension fund with defined benefits, so it should not be maximising returns. When it did try to maximise returns, it went from being 99%-funded to 90%-funded in the crash. There was *no need* for it, because it is a defined-benefit fund. The surplus should be put into bonds, not shares.)

Whoever controls resources has a strong influence on the production structure, although the structure of demand also affects capital. The capital relationship is a central determinant of economic direction and must be managed strategically. Two things follow from this. First, narrow BEE is an important consideration as, in many ways, it represents the government's only policy on capital. How important is creating a more representative capitalist class? Second, is *broad-based* BEE (BBBEE) a response that works? Would broad-based shareholding, employee ownership plans and community trusts change decision-making in the economy towards greater equity and access to resources? Alternatively, what about enhancing competition where it is viable? What does this imply for meeting the needs of companies to become internationally competitive? A third alternative would be to develop new sectors, which would, in turn, develop new kinds of capital. If South Africa could develop the kind of economic activity that promotes smaller firms and greater competition, would that help to restructure power in the economy? These three options can obviously be combined, but is broad-based ownership of large companies is really a solution? Or even, if it were the second-best solution, is it the 'best second-best'? In mining, the government is driving extremely narrow BEE at a massive cost to the economy. What else could be done about mining capital? The mining industry needs support, especially since it appears to be struggling just before the new economy is being built.

The state has a responsibility, given its limited resources, to support particular sectors. It must clearly support exports but this must be balanced with the needs of the domestic market. The sectors that can create more employment tend to be oriented towards domestic and regional markets rather than the international markets, because of productivity issues. The government has neither the capacity nor has it allocated the responsibility within the state to support domestic industry. Consider construction, which had long been a major job creator: no one in government is responsible for ensuring that the industry is maximised in a way that creates decent work. The same holds for the retail sector, which is the largest single employer and has a major impact through backward linkages to manufacturing and agriculture. Despite its huge impact on the real economy, the dti has not allocated the responsibility for the sector to dedicated staff because it does not see retail as part of the 'real' economy.

The development of new industries is often blocked simply because no infrastructure has been developed for them. This is an important lever for the state, but it is seldom used because the agencies that provide infrastructure are separate from those that make economic policy. The core functions of the state can be used to encourage new industries where there are gaps, provided that these functions are aligned with a core industrial strategy.

2. Elements of the structure and drivers of change

Charlotte du Toit

This presentation examines the structure of the economy and particularly focuses on ways for the state to intervene. It presents a framework and a set of guidelines that should inform policy interventions to change the structure of the economy. The presentation covers five points:

1. Restate the problem.
2. Understand its core and nature.
3. Identify the structure of the economy and the drivers of change (the 'engine room').
4. Design solutions for dealing with the structural problem.
5. Evaluate policy approaches and challenges – how can the state intervene?

South Africa has successfully transformed its political environment but this has not been accompanied by an economic transformation. It is still 'business as usual' and the policy rules of the Washington Consensus still hold sway. This must be revisited: are these rules applicable to South Africa? Are they needed for the sake of credibility with the 'big players'? Is the country dealing with its unique problems? Through the Washington Consensus policies of targeting economic stability through monetary and fiscal policy, South Africa has managed to accelerate economic growth. However, this growth has been outpaced by the rate of growth of new entrants to the labour market.

As a result, the level of inequality as measured by the Gini coefficient has not improved. In fact the distribution of income has worsened despite the growth of the economy. If anything, there has been a sideways movement or even a deterioration in the distribution of income. Related to this is evidence that remuneration as a percentage of total income has fallen. This means that households, individuals and consumers are sharing less and less in the income that is generated by this economy, while more is taken by domestic and foreign businesses. This is linked to the issue of portfolio investment: this is indeed an inflow of capital, some of which may find its way towards productive investment. However, since it is subject to high risks in the economy, there have to be returns in the form of dividend and interest payments. Dividend and interest outflows are growing exponentially, to alarming levels, and pose a risk on the balance of payments.

Therefore, while income has grown over time, it is not finding its way to households and individuals. This has worsened inequality and is making little, if any, dent in poverty levels. Evidence shows that most poverty alleviation came from grant transfers rather than the core operations of the economy.

This problem can be simplified as follows: does the structural constraint lie in the lack of spending, or with capacity constraints that do not respond to accelerated spending? This question has a fundamental bearing on economic policy. Are the lack of employment and the persistence of poverty and inequality due to insufficient demand, as is often argued? Or, in contrast, is the core problem the opposite? Does the supply (production capacity) not respond to demand and spending behaviour?

The international response to the global recession has been to target spending and the lack of demand. The idea was to put money into the pockets of individuals in order to restore their spending, which would 'automatically' generate a response from the production side of the economy. However, even the World Bank now believes that the recession was not simply the result of a poor regulatory framework in financial markets. Instead, it argues that countries have been outpacing their economic capacity and, to achieve sustainable growth in the long run, these capacity constraints in the global economy must be addressed.

The fundamental difference is whether structural constraints are seen to be on the demand (spending) or the supply (capacity) side. On the one hand, various policy tools can be used to facilitate spending, which should raise demand and ultimately result in higher production from the domestic industrial environment. Higher production is based on higher employment and investment, which allows the owners of capital goods, labour and skills to participate in the productive economy with earned incomes. The fundamental effectiveness of this approach relies on the capacity of domestic production to respond to the increase in demand. However, when there are capacity constraints in the economy, firms will not respond with additional production to supply the higher demand, regardless of whether that demand is foreign or domestic. There is a debate about targeting export or domestic markets, but where there are structural capacity constraints, domestic firms will not share in the income because they do not have access to the investment, skills or technology needed to respond to the higher demand.

The fundamental operations of an effective economy are to grow and employ its labour and physical resources effectively so that income is shared and there is equity and relative wealth across all spheres of society. On the one side are supply and the productive capacity. On the other is demand: the people who need to buy and the goods and services that need to be distributed. The process works through various transfer mechanisms and a set of prices that regulates the flow of these goods and services. This is the real economy, the engine room through which income and GDP are generated, jobs are created and resources are employed.

What is fundamental to this capacity? On the productive side, the long-term structure of the economy is based on three pillars: capital goods, resource allocation and institutional frameworks. How productive are the processes that combine natural and labour resources with the capital stock and infrastructure? This is reflected in investment in capital goods and resource allocation, and how these are combined in a productive, effective way through technologies, processes and institutional frameworks. On the demand side, there are also three pillars of income or buying power through which the government may intervene. Buying power can be generated by selling resources, using credit and funding, or obtaining transfers from abroad, from domestic sources (e.g. inheritances) or from the state.

What are the constraints, the labour issues, the capital and investment issues and the productivity issues? How do they relate to one another? Figure 2.1 presents a streamlined framework of the structure of the economy, the constraints and the angles for intervention. These elements do not operate in isolation. The institutional environment influences the effectiveness of the interaction between capacity and demand: how prices are formed or distorted, transfers are conducted, credit and money flow, income is generated through participation, and technology is accumulated. It also influences how productive the economy is, how accessible the labour market is and how capital and investment could contribute to increasing the capacity of the economy.

In assessing the institutional environment and the potential for the government to play a significant role, the institutional role players must be identified. Which institutions and businesses play a significant role in this environment? Who are the political role players and the individual consumers? Which

Figure 2.1: Economic structure

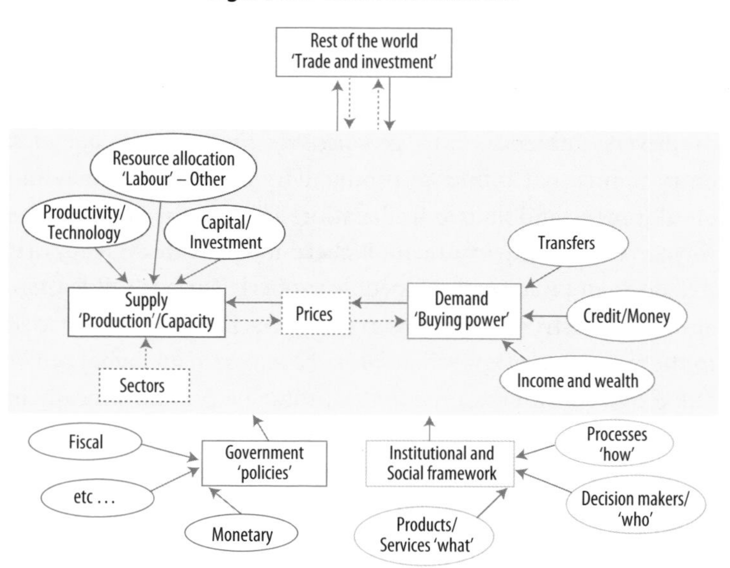

processes could be influenced and what is their institutional environment? The institutional environment includes the flow of information, coalitions and monopolies, how prices are set and whether rigidities in administered prices distort the price structure. What products and services are produced? Do they meet demand? Another factor of great importance in the South African institutional environment is the role of the rest of the world in finance flows, via trade and other channels. These issues all affect the way the economy operates to ensure sustainable incomes. The structure in Figure 2.1 is a checklist for potential policy interventions. It highlights the constraints within the institutional framework that is supposed to facilitate economic effectiveness, and assists in identifying opportunities for state intervention.

The final element of the structure is the contribution of the state, using a range of policies and tools. What tools are available? Is the government using them effectively? Is it targeting the right entry points? In designing where the government should intervene and how this needs to be phased in, rigorous information is fundamentally important.

What are the core drivers of the economy? The first set of drivers influences how *productively the economy operates:* entry points that influence productivity relate to research and development, and skills and education. These in turn relate to the socio-economic environment. Is there adequate health support? Are poor and marginalised people properly supported? Is there enough infrastructure such as roads and schools? Is there access to the right *technology*? What *has to be imported* and what *can be found locally*? How can the bulk of these be provided locally in future?

The second set of drivers reflects the *resource allocation* of employment and physical resources. On the supply side, entry points include:

(a) *Skills:* How effective is the education system as an incubator of skills? This relates to the socio-economic environment and the availability of tools, infrastructure, roads, and the like.
(b) *Beneficiation:* Are resources used to their full potential, with the latest technologies, to create economies of scale?
(c) *Accessibility:* Are the resources accessible?
(d) *Flexibility:* How responsive is the market to short-term constraints?

The third set of drivers relates to *investment* or the capital stock of the economy. What funding is available, whether local or foreign? Is enough funding available through the institutional framework? What is the cost of investment, and what role should the government play in that? What is the implication of this cost for monetary policy and inflation targeting? Does that not imply a trade-off? For example, when inflation is structural in nature, it may persist when demand is lowered, because of monopolies or high administered or imported prices. Local monetary policy has no impact on these factors and inflation targeting in such a situation would lower both production and income and, therefore, the growth potential of the economy. Access to investment funding is also pertinent to the institutional framework. Is it only available to high-income groups? What investment funding is available to small and medium firms, which are a core component of the production structure? How attractive is the economy to foreign investors? How competitive is it?

Based on this institutional framework, a series of constraints is linked to these drivers: market responsiveness; how prices are formed; information flow or the lack thereof; how the transmission processes take place; and the institutional and regulatory frameworks.

Given the three sets of drivers, the economy has to operate under a capacity ceiling while trying to generate sufficient income to lower poverty. As Figures 2.2 and 2.3 show, the challenge is to raise that ceiling, ensuring that sufficient income is generated to enable role players to participate in this process with earned incomes. That is the solution as a core set, and it is fully in line with the Polokwane resolutions. To get participation in the productive economy with an earned and sustainable income, the ceiling must be raised over time.

Figure 2.2: The growth

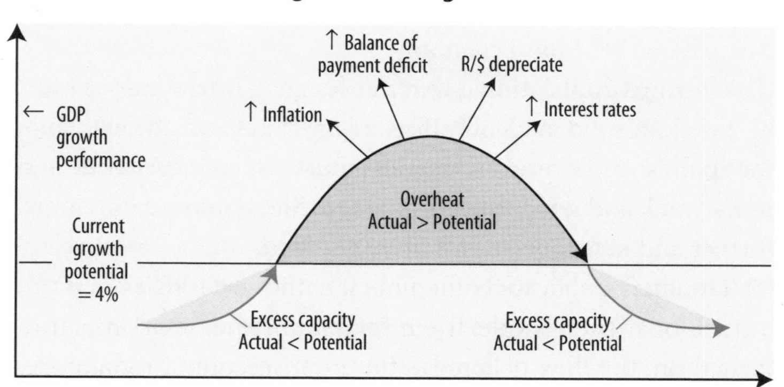

Figure 2.3: Raising the growth ceiling

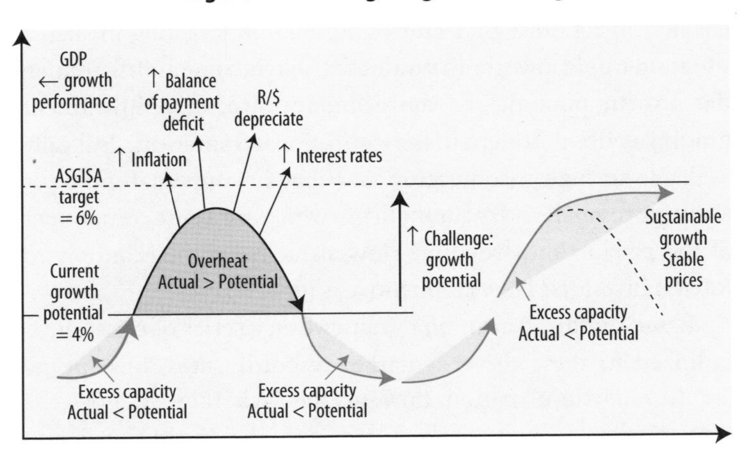

What are the implications for policy? The first is to target the drivers of change. There is a distinction between sustainable long-run drivers of capacity (those that influence productivity, resource allocation and investment) and rescue packages to smooth an interim downswing. 'Raising the ceiling' targets the long-term capacity of income. The short-run package simply bridges the adjustment process on the way to raising production capacity.

The second implication is the need for a multi-dimensional and integrated approach. None of this can be done in isolation. There are always interactions that create winners and losers. There are always buyers and providers, and foreigners who participate in the local economy.

The third implication is that the design of interventions must be based on solid evidence. If necessary, based on the evidence, the policy tools and strategies must be reprioritised and redesigned, and good aspects retained. Some may be developed further and new tools may well be required.

The final implication for policy is the need to address the institutional framework: the responsiveness of markets, price formation, the flow of information, transmission mechanisms, the regulatory system, infrastructure and the capacity to support effective service delivery.

Fundamentally, the idea is not to target spending power in the long run in the belief that this will translate into employment creation. None of this will happen before the country has dealt with the bottlenecks and constraints on the supply side.

Discussion

> *Neva Makgetla noted that a structuralist approach involves active engagement by the state to change the structure of production, and is not confined to crosscutting interventions. Does this framework go beyond supply, demand and crosscutting issues to deal with being a resource-based economy? What is the vision for the economy, for its ownership and control?*

The framework is not only about supply and demand but also about the institutional framework that facilitates these. A focus on the supply side will raise the income potential, which will facilitate higher and sustainable spending and demand. Future work on the high-level framework will look at issues such as productive capacity, industry, the institutional environment, ownership and control, available resources, global influences, and how these are interlinked. None of these can be seen in isolation.

It is ultimately about productive capacity. What are the revealed comparative advantages of the various sectors? Based on the evidence, where must the state assist? What does this imply for industrial, trade and other policies? What are the impediments to productive capacity? There is substantial evidence to indicate that a focus on productive capacity, and on the institutional support to facilitate it, will raise the growth potential and increase the basket of goods and income that can be shared.

3. The changing structure of the South African economy

Jorge Maia

The structure of the South African economy has changed progressively over the years. Figure 3.1 shows the broad sectoral composition of the economy over more than 60 years. The changes in the past decade or so have clearly been significant.

The economy is increasingly dominated by the services sectors, which is in line with trends especially in the advanced economies. The primary sectors – agriculture and mining – have seen their shares of the GDP fall substantially over the past five decades. The share of the manufacturing sector, which is the second largest in the economy, has decreased sharply since the early 1990s. This followed South Africa's reintegration into the global community, the subsequent trade liberalisation process, the competitive forces of globalisation and the increasingly challenging environment for global trade.

Over time, the relative contribution in the mining sector to GDP declined and the composition of its output changed as gold production fell and the platinum subsector grew. The secondary sectors, especially manufacturing, also saw significant change: a deindustrialisation trend began in the 1990s and continued into the new millennium. The tertiary sectors grew dramatically in this period, with significant implications for employment, the production of tradables and the balance of payments, among others. The services sector

Figure 3.1: Structure of the South African economy, 1946 to 2008

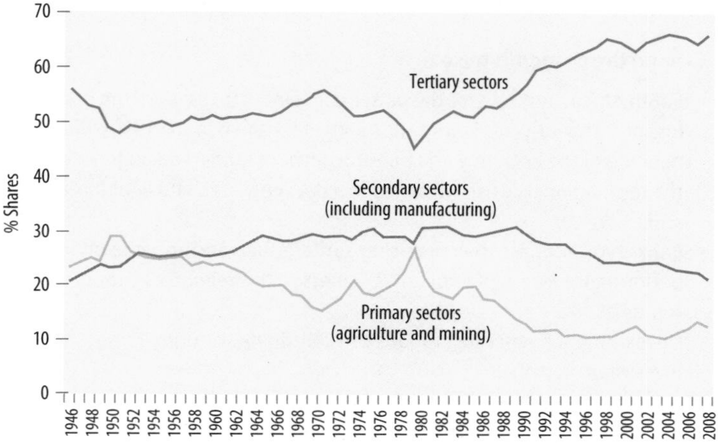

Source: SARB

itself changed with the rapid expansion of subsectors such as telecommunications.

Fixed investment showed solid annual growth until the onset of the global economic crisis. On a sectoral level, the services sectors dominated, especially financial services, transport, storage and communication services and, more recently, electricity. The contribution of the 'productive' sectors was more muted, although manufacturing made significant contributions in specific years.

This is problematic: the economy is increasingly dominated by the services sectors and investment in its productive base, including the industrial sectors, is inadequate. This has adverse implications for the balance of payments as South Africa relies more heavily on foreign savings to finance its deficits. This becomes a constraint as soon as investment activity accelerates, owing to the high import requirements of fixed investment projects.

Future directions

Table 3.1 may be rather simplistic but it attempts to capture the needs of the South African economy.

Table 3.1: Towards a radically different South African economy by 2025

Expand the economic base

- South Africa must reverse the pattern of deindustrialisation (the gradual loss of competitiveness since the 1980s, intensified in the 1990s with the opening of the economy and phasing down of tariffs, and aggravated in the recent global crisis), which led to a decline in its share of global GDP and trade.
- Banks typically base their financing authorisation and appetite on the performance record of applicant businesses; this reinforces current trends.
- Development finance institutions can contribute to augmenting investment activity in:
  - Improving competitiveness through new technologies that will lead to an expansion of industry and of small and medium enterprises
  - New industries, such as renewable energy, resource beneficiation and advanced manufacturing
  - Future industries, such as smart materials, bio- and nanotechnology
  - Large projects with substantial potential for forward and backward linkages and value addition
  - Leveraging current and future capital expenditure programmes, whether public, private, regional or national.

Alter the trajectory of the economy

- The current structural trajectory needs to be changed.
- The momentum of gross fixed capital formation in recent years has been towards construction and services, propelled by credit-driven consumer spending and rising incomes, which are cyclical and even unsustainable.
- The financial sector has typically been comfortable with such investment, which often entails asset-backed (real estate) security.
- Investment in the mining sector has been strong but falls short of significant beneficiation.
- Investment allocation must be balanced between enabling production and servicing consumers, local consumption and exports, tradables and non-tradables, and job creation and capital intensity.
- The economy must leverage regional resources.
- Value chains need further development (in terms of both depth and breadth) while understanding the different characteristics and merits of individual segments of the value chain, whether capital- or labour-intensive.

Change the ownership structure of the economy

- Inequalities are not being addressed at an acceptable pace; the current situation is not sustainable and is potentially explosive.
- Discrepancies are demographic, as well as regional (provincial), rural-urban and intra-urban.
- The participant/beneficiary base of BEE must be 'massified'.
- Entrepreneurial development must be provided to the historically disadvantaged. The state can contribute to job creation and upskilling through conditionalities associated with state incentives and funding.

Conceptualise and work towards a 'desirable' economy by 2025

Labour-absorbing, value-adding, regionally integrated, innovation-driven, globally competitive and greener economy.

First, South Africa's productive base must be expanded and the deindustrialisation pattern reversed. This gradual loss in competitiveness started with the sanctions in the 1980s and intensified in the 1990s when the opening of the economy exposed a general lack of competitiveness. South Africa's manufacturing sector was unprepared for the lowering of import protection as tariffs were often reduced at a faster pace or to levels lower than those agreed upon with the World Trade Organization. This was compounded by the appreciation of the currency after the commodities boom: the strength of the rand since 2002 has been a significant factor in the deindustrialisation of the economy. The recent global economic crisis aggravated this process as global and domestic demand plummeted and competition increased when companies scrambled to capture local and export markets.

A core objective of a development finance institution such as the Industrial Development Corporation (IDC) is to address market gaps left by the private financial sector. In their financing decisions, commercial banks are typically driven by the track record of applicant businesses. Consequently, their financing activities tend to reinforce historical trends. They are often reluctant to finance new or emerging industries, or even greenfield projects. This stance can change quite swiftly once the new industries prove attractive to the private financial sector.

There is a clear need to augment investment activity, especially in labour-intensive industries that have the potential to expand in areas where the country holds comparative or competitive advantages. Competitiveness can be improved by upgrading production capacity, raising productivity levels and introducing new technologies, while promoting employment preservation and growth. South Africa also needs to phase out obsolete approaches that contribute to industrial stagnation; renovate the existing production base, particularly in manufacturing; and introduce new industries.

In facing up to these enormous challenges, South Africa cannot afford to be left behind. It needs to catch up swiftly or it will lag behind the global economy within a decade or two. It must add value to resources, develop advanced manufacturing and introduce new technologies. These include the green industries that support the rapid growth of renewable and alternative energy, as well as smart materials, cleaner technologies and bio- and nanotechnologies. Some of these 'industries of tomorrow' will provide a momentum resembling that of the information and communication technology (ICT) sector in the past decade. They have a massive potential for growing the economic base and creating employment. Other countries are exploiting these developments quite aggressively, even clearly incentivising the change under the guise of stimulating economic recovery.

Large project developments tend to be capital-intensive, leading many to wonder if they are worth pursuing. However, they have numerous forward and backward linkages, as well as positive attributes such as adding value, generating export earnings or substituting imports.

Economic players need to leverage off the public sector's ongoing capital expenditure programme, maximising the opportunities for local procurement. South Africa has already missed several opportunities to localise during the unfolding of the government's massive investment programme. This is reflected in a growing import bill.

The current structural trajectory of the economy must be altered. In recent years, gross capital formation has gravitated towards the services sectors, fuelled by and further stimulating the demand side of the economy. One of the main problems highlighted by the global crisis – and South Africa is no exception – is that demand has been pushed towards unsustainable levels.

This does not apply to the entire population: many people are still being marginalised by the financial sector. However, it certainly applies to those who have traditionally had access to credit. Unsustainable household indebtedness has had an adverse effect on the balance of payment through the purchase of foreign consumer goods, including luxury items. The changes in the composition of South Africa's import basket in recent years reflect a shift towards luxury goods and consumables that the country may well be unable to afford. This behaviour must be altered; hopefully, this reality is setting in as consumers recognise the need to reduce the levels of both demand and debt.

Before the crisis, the credit-driven consumption in South Africa was stimulated by a fast-growing financial services sector, backed by rising incomes and asset prices. This pattern increased the cyclicality of the system, as well as its unsustainability. The financial sector is, of course, usually comfortable with this type of funding or investment activity, as long as asset prices continue to rise.

Investment in mining has been strong but it has fallen well short of any significant beneficiation. This needs to be addressed, as the country cannot afford to perpetuate the exportation of largely unbeneficiated mineral resources.

Future investment should strike a better balance between labour- and capital-intensive activities, between production-enabling and consumer servicing activities, between production for the local and the export markets, and between tradable and non-tradable goods. This does not mean that one is better than the other; it is simply a call for more balance. The huge imbalances of recent years have created serious economic and social problems for both present and future generations.

Value chains need to be substantially developed, both locally and regionally, in depth and breadth. South Africa falls short in this regard and its Asian counterparts, among other foreign investors, have recognised this gap. Chinese or Indian investors, for instance, have shown an increasing interest in extracting the natural resource wealth of Africa in order to develop value chains back home. Africa's economies and peoples are losing out on this enormous potential. It is important to leverage the continent's resources and create globally competitive value chains at the regional level, beyond national borders. The time has come to develop well-integrated regional economies on the African continent.

Ownership

Lastly, the ownership structure of the South African economy must change to address prevailing inequalities. This legacy is not only demographic but also spatial, in terms of regions, provinces, and rural-urban and intra-urban discrepancies. The pace of change in ownership has been far too slow – this is potentially explosive. It is critical to expand the beneficiary base beyond the narrow one that has characterised the BEE process until recently.

South Africa needs to focus on entrepreneurial development, particularly among historically disadvantaged communities. This is vital for the transformation of society. Emerging entrepreneurs need considerable support, especially if they engage in productive and job-creating activities. Employment creation and skills development are imperatives that should be reflected in the conditionalities associated with state incentives, financing and other forms of support.

Towards a radically different economy

The economy that South Africa desires to develop in years to come (with 2025 as an arbitrary target year) would be labour-intensive, greener, innovative, competitive in the global economy and integrated into the region, and would add high levels of value. This is a vision of the economy to work towards in changing the old and building the new.

Discussion: A way forward

This discussion focused on priorities for the second seminar in the series, building on the findings of the first seminar. Participants suggested that, instead of just outlining a vision and process for the economy, there was a need to identify real priorities, the linkages between them and their affordability.

A primary concern is the impact of the structure of capital, as well as of production and ownership. Decision-making in the economy is, in effect, in the private sector. Decisions made by the private sector create the objective structure of production, but are also influenced by it.

The next seminar should clarify exactly what is meant by structure, including the real economy (agriculture, mining and manufacturing) and the services sector (including financial services). It needs to define the structure of the economy and its components, outline the vision for the structure, review the various available tools and examine how to design coherent and integrated policies to achieve the desired structure. This could include exploring issues of value addition in these sectors, such as, for instance, why entrepreneurs are reluctant to invest in manufacturing.

In order to design a long-term vision for the economy, the

current structure must be properly analysed in terms of its potential for value addition and employment creation. Every sector should be assessed based on its ownership and control, patterns of production and distribution, and the spatial dimension. This will assist in identifying a vision, the steps for attaining it and the tools for attempting the required changes. There is also a question of sequencing these steps.

Participants will be asked to identify the three key interventions required to leverage the desired structural change: *If there were three things to change in government economic or social policy, what would they be? Which three specific things should be added or removed?*

Part Two

Value Addition in the Real Economy

Opening remarks

Ben Turok

Objectives

This seminar focused on proposals to ensure *value addition and the potential for decent work*, especially in manufacturing, mining and agriculture. Many developing countries have failed to grow their share of global value chains by advancing into higher-level functions. In part, this is because of the financialisation of the world economy and the concentration of economic power, which enables international corporations to control global value chains and limit developing countries to the lowest-value functions.

In South Africa, the financialisation of the economy has contributed to high levels of economic concentration and a skewed development path. Large interventions by finance houses have undermined industry by fuelling a debt-driven consumer boom based on imports. Inflows of foreign capital consist mainly of portfolio investments that may cause bubbles in the economy, while net foreign direct investment is small and limited to particular areas.

The concentration of ownership and control in most industries is as high as it was before 1994. If the government is to intervene in the path of industrialisation, it has to identify the locus of power in the main value chains. Any such intervention will require substantial political will.

The challenge is great as several sectors are relatively stagnant. For instance, the capital stock in manufacturing has not grown for some time and there has been relative deindustrialisation since 1994, except in the automotive industry. Hence, the economy is growing increasingly dependent on its primary physical resources.

Rent extraction from the productive sectors has been channelled into credit rather than fixed investment. This, in turn, has fuelled the expansion of the wholesale and retail sectors, as well as imports, thereby worsening the trade balance and current account. Over the last 15 years, there has been much rent-seeking behaviour that lobbied for special privileges from the state and extracted value without building productive capacity or contributing to overall wealth, employment or well-being.

With the three main productive sectors of the economy stagnant, the question becomes: what can be expected to be the engine of the economy? What will be the drivers of growth and jobs?

Manufacturing

Manufacturing is a strong candidate for the following reasons:

1. It is scalable with higher proportional returns to investment, as there are strong multipliers.
2. More investment leads to more employment – a vital consideration in South Africa.
3. It has scope for productivity and income growth over time through better technologies and management techniques.
4. Growth is feasible in areas with medium barriers to entry and where there are complementarities between investment and productivity. There is also a natural advantage in making or beneficiating products where transport costs are a significant

proportion of final costs (for example, paper rather than jewellery).

The key levers for a shift in direction are:

1. A change to a more favourable macroeconomic policy
2. Localisation and procurement using the economic strength of the state, such as tendering in favour of local component manufacturing
3. Large-scale concessionary financing for industry by the state and related institutions, such as from the Unemployment Insurance Fund and the Government Employees Pension Fund, and delivered through institutions such as the IDC.

Additional measures include:

1. Trade policy (appropriate tariff and non-tariff barriers and export taxes)
2. Competition policy to reduce commodity prices in monopoly sectors
3. A review of BEE, which has failed to create black-owned productive enterprises
4. Massive skills development
5. Expansion of industrial energy

Among the priorities are:

1. Beneficiation (e.g. of forestry products, to produce paper rather than export pulp)
2. Domestic supply of components (e.g. produce more bulky materials and components for automotive assembly operations)
3. Rebuilding capacity in tooling and capital equipment, including foundries and mechanical engineering

4. Building heavy commercial vehicles
5. Agro-processing
6. Green industries
7. Manufacturing durable consumer goods, such as furniture.

South Africa could develop competitive advantages in all of these sectors.

Mining

The two main mining complexes in South Africa are on the Witwatersrand and in the Bushveld. Mining is mostly a mature industry, although it still makes a significant contribution to the economy. Mineral resources are substantial, in some cases the largest in the world. Mining contributes only 8% of GDP but earns about 33% of export revenues. Unlike in the golden years of apartheid, it now contributes little to tax revenue.

The processing of minerals follows the sequence from extraction and primary processing to manufacture and product creation. Simple beneficiation is done in South Africa, while higher levels of beneficiation, such as manufacturing gold and diamond jewellery, are done abroad. High-level beneficiation is not easy: it requires good linkages, design capabilities and market sensitivity. The side-stream effects of mining, such as infrastructure and human resource development, are also important for South Africa.

It has to be recognised that mining is a wasting resource, and multipliers are difficult to achieve. Furthermore, the offshore listing of mining companies such as Anglo American has led to the externalisation of much of the country's research and development capability and related manufacturing. But, in partnership with mining companies, the government may be able to identify niche areas with potential for beneficiation, such as basic jewellery rather than high-end fashion products.

Agriculture

Contrary to conventional wisdom, agriculture is not just about farming. The agro-food value chain includes an upstream and downstream to agriculture, which strongly influence the nature of farming and are often highly concentrated. Supermarkets and fast foods are good examples of this. Fast food influences consumer choice in favour of meat, especially poultry, at the expense of balanced diets. In this way, consumption determines production. Supermarkets put pressure on retailers and wholesalers through centralised procurement, and farmers receive very little. Farming inputs are also subject to high levels of concentration, leading to high input costs. Higher food prices thus benefit retailers more than producers and subsidies go to corporations, not farmers.

International corporations integrate the global food markets. They promote particular forms of farming, such as the production of grain for livestock instead of grass. In many countries, particularly the United States, these activities are subsidised by the government.

That said, there are still considerable possibilities for increased local production. If Kenya can supply 40% of all cut flowers sold in the Netherlands, South Africa can find other niche areas beyond wine and apples.

Conclusions

Evidence shows that value added is low in the real economy, leading to unemployment and thus poverty. On the other hand, rent seeking is pervasive, explaining the high levels of inequality and the indifferent overall performance of the economy. If correct, this has serious implications for policymakers in the ANC and the state. Among these are:

- Solutions based on 'inclusive growth' may be unrealistic: inclusion in a stagnant real economy is problematic.

- Incremental adjustments to the social wage are important but inadequate and unsustainable without real increases in production.

The following questions arise:

- Is lowering the cost of doing business an adequate response without reforming the structure of the economy?
- Are the ANC and the government bold enough to tackle the inherited economic structure?
- Are they bold enough to confront capital? Are there serious alternatives?
- Can major changes be made before social tensions rise further?
- Can the government invigorate the public service for improved delivery?
- Can the state devise substantial means of job creation, which go beyond outsourced low-paid jobs, the security industry, retail and personal services, and other insecure and peripheral jobs?

The analysis thus far shows that the role of the state and its institutions is grossly underestimated. A strong and substantial state is vital in a capitalist economy as a counterweight to the private sector. The role of the state is to:

1. Provide investment financing on a massive scale.
2. Be the largest procurer of goods and services of all kinds.
3. Provide employment on a large scale.
4. Provide physical infrastructure to facilitate business growth.
5. Develop the human capital and skills that are vital inputs to the economy.
6. Regulate the economy to prevent inefficiencies and speculative activity, and promote decent working conditions.
7. Rely on commercial banks to lubricate the financial sector.

The analysis also emphasises that South Africa's biggest problem is the massive underclass, which has poor prospects under present policies. To address the needs of the underclass, the country will have to find ways of expanding its utilisation of financial, physical and human resources. That is the subject of the next seminar.

4. Improving the performance of manufacturing

Simon Roberts

This presentation deals with changing the path of industrialisation. Outcomes such as value creation and employment depend on the development path that is followed. To make more than incremental changes to these outcomes, long-term measures are needed to fundamentally alter that path.

A principal aspect of the development path is the decisions of large firms. Small firms are affected by the decisions of large firms. In every sector, such as manufacturing or agriculture, the value chain tends to be governed by large firms. 'Govern' can mean control through setting standards within the retail chain, accessing inputs or benefiting from bottlenecks. It is important to understand where the power lies in a value chain and how that affects people's ability to participate, as well as the distribution of returns from activities throughout the value chain. This is particularly true in South Africa, more so than in many other economies, because the economy is highly concentrated as a result of previous government intervention (and non-intervention). The development path is also affected by macroeconomic and financial sector policies.

There are choices that can be made about the development path and are in fact being made; even not choosing is a choice. Government choices on industrial policy must be understood in terms of changing the decisions of firms to yield collectively better outcomes. Government decision-making has improved through the Industrial Policy Action Plans (IPAPs). The latest one, IPAP 2, is both more ambitious and clearer about the desired outcomes. Political will, leadership, coordination and the levers that will be used are critical to its success, as are measures to be taken by the government as a whole.

The problem can be summarised as follows: South Africa's overall performance has been poor, especially where it matters most (investment and employment). The economy is fragile and structurally weak. The development path is skewed owing to both intervention by the apartheid state and the resource base of the economy. More recently, the financial sector has driven much of the development path, particularly the consumption-led growth over the past decade or so. The inherited development path has the following characteristics:

- The minerals-energy complex has set the agenda.
- The exchange rate reflects minerals endowment and cheap energy rather than productive capabilities and the potential for diversifying the industry.
- Trade liberalisation has merely entrenched the existing static comparative advantages instead of supporting dynamic advantages.
- The financial sector is oriented to consumption rather than productive investment.
- There is a fundamental misunderstanding of what growth in services may mean and how sustainable it is.

Concerted industrial policies are required to alter this growth path. South Africa is ignoring the lessons of comparative development that were learnt in the past 14 years, even those drawn by orthodox economists.

Some sectors are drivers on the production side; they invest in productive capabilities. Other sectors are driven largely by

Figure 4.1: Economic growth per sector, 1994 to 2008

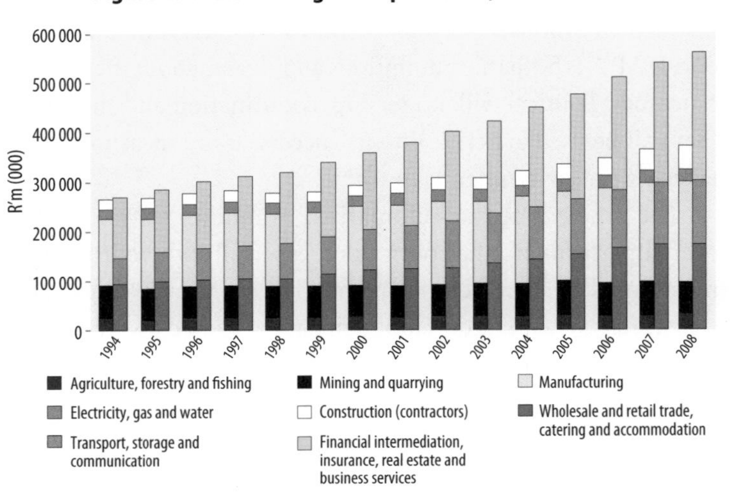

consumption and by particular groups in society. The growth of these sectors over time is shown in Figure 4.1. In the figure, the right-hand side of each stack shows the consumption side of the economy. It grew strongly in the last decade because the upper and middle classes were flush with cash during the boom in credit and residential housing prices. Such growth is unsustainable but, while it lasted, wholesale and retail trade grew strongly and created many jobs. These jobs are now being lost.

The second consumption sector is transport, logistics and telecommunications. Logistics and transport are derived amounts since they depend on the production of goods to transport. The growth in telecommunications reflects a change in consumption patterns. Clearly, people are spending a higher portion of their incomes in this sector, consuming more internet and related services. Despite the growth in the sector, South Africa has been unable to generate self-standing telecommunications activities, such as business process outsourcing.

The last consumption sector is financial services. The question is whether the growth of the financial services sector is due to speculative or derivative activity, or whether it is servicing investment and productive capacity. Much of the growth in investment has been in speculative activities: lending for housing, speculating on the South African Futures Exchange (SAFEX) and the like.

Contrast the growth in these sectors with the growth in productive activity in agriculture, mining and manufacturing. Manufacturing is the largest of these sectors and should be the focus area for building the productive side of the economy. Figure 4.1 frames the debate in this regard. It shows that the retail sector is a sound vehicle for people to distribute their production to the market or to buy and consume. Concentration in retail *is* a problem, however, because smaller producers cannot get their products to the market and rural communities have to travel into towns to find retailers.

Within the manufacturing sector, only resource-based activities and the automotive sector have been growing, as shown in Figure 4.2. This implies that the only non-resource activity with any growth is the only sector that had an industrial policy after 1994. Everything else that is growing is based on resources. The resource-based sectors are the products of industrial policy under apartheid; they are the apartheid era's infant industries that have grown up. The automotive sector is the only sector that had a comprehensive-apartheid industrial policy.

Much of this growth has been driven by short-term capital, which created liquidity in the local financial markets. This, in turn, stimulated consumption and speculation. This is the story of the South African economy: the driver of growth is short-term speculative financial inflows.

Figure 4.3 examines exports. Trade is an exchange: when South Africa exports large volumes of unbeneficiated resources, it imports many manufactured items. It is important to understand that trade is not 'win-win'. In terms of the trade balance, when there is a big trade surplus in one sector, another

Figure 4.2: Growth in manufacturing, 1994 to 2008 (1994 base year)

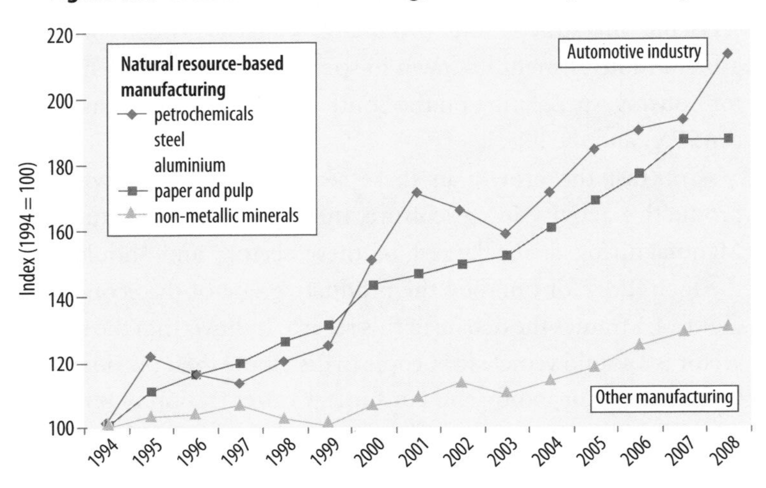

sector is negatively affected. A country needs to make choices about its pattern of trade. These choices are linked to choices about its pattern of industrial development (or non-choices, in the case of South Africa).

In the figure, 'basic chemicals' is essentially just Sasol, and 'basic iron and steel' and 'basic non-ferrous metals' represent just three companies. These companies have been allocated electricity at a price that is lower than the cost of its production. South Africa's non-choices in this regard are really choices for the continued privilege of sectors that had been supported before. There is path dependence too: these companies have significant infrastructure and considerable political influence.

The remaining sectors include, first, motor vehicles. While exports in this sector have grown, so have imports (and possibly at a higher rate). Second is 'other goods', such as furniture, textiles and clothing, all of which can generate employment. South Africa could and should also produce inputs for the infrastructure programme, such as fabricated metal products, capital equipment and transport equipment.

Figure 4.3: Merchandise exports, 1990 to 2008

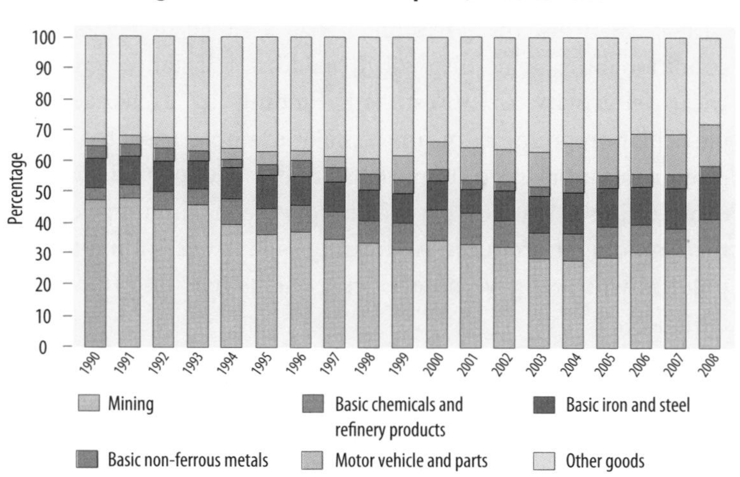

Who benefits in terms of the capital stock? The government is the largest sector, followed by business services and finance, other mining, transport and storage, communication, trade, and electricity and gas. Only then does the manufacturing sector appear. This, the sector that South Africa needs to grow, has not changed its capital stock. In fact, as in other industrialising or developing countries, manufacturing has suffered most from the recession. Activity in the manufacturing sector has declined to levels last seen in 2004.

Concentration levels in the industrial structure remain as high as ever, despite the unbundling within the conglomerates. Anglo American's share of the industry has declined significantly but its unbundling of selected subsidiaries does not imply that the level of concentration within these industries has fallen; it may even be increasing. BEE has reinforced the patterns of concentration because, with few exceptions, it has involved buying into larger groups rather than creating new entrants.

The big firms are even stronger because they have internationalised with offshore listings but that does not mean that they are beyond the reach of the state. In its engagement with large firms, the government has a range of levers and conditionalities at its disposal. It could, for instance, provide cheap electricity or investment funding in exchange for particular programmes or projects. For example, Sasol has been given substantial state support to build a new petrochemicals complex in the Waterberg, yet it charges the maximum price for the ammonia it produces. Addressing such issues is a matter of political will, and government departments may find this hard to handle.

A developmental state is less about coordination than it is about *having the will to engage with large firms and to understand what drives their decisions.* South Korea achieved this. Even the World Bank's Commission on Growth and Development (2008: 9), chaired by Michael Spence (a Nobel laureate in economics), advised that resource-based economies 'will only improve on this sorry historical record if they capture an appropriate share of the resource rents; save a judicious amount overseas; and set clear, growth-oriented priorities for absorbing the remainder at home.' The report also warns against subsidising electricity, except to supply vulnerable sections of society.

South Africa's trade performance reflects past capabilities and liberalisation has reinforced these patterns. The country should be looking at building future capabilities instead. Liberalisation claims to create a 'level playing field' but it is level only for the teams with the best players, because they have all the money. In the South African context, the best teams are firms like ArcelorMittal. Since the government built their plants, they will obviously win export markets. In contrast, many smaller firms do not receive support.

The Harvard Panel, which was appointed by the government and which reported in 2008, contends that liberalisation is associated with diversification. It is not. What diversification took place resulted from the Motor Industry Development

Programme (MIDP) and its effects beyond the automotive sector: within capital equipment, it was catalytic converters; within rubber products, it was tyres. *Diversification came from intervention, not liberalisation.*

Trade policy involves making structural choices. In any economy, the development of capabilities is path dependent, and changing the path requires strong incentives and intervention. Trade policy is the easiest way to alter relative prices, through both import tariffs and export duties, and it is (implicitly) linked to performance. Since it favours one sector over another, it induces structural change.

From a trade point of view, the markets for the industries that the country wants to develop are much more likely to be in the region than overseas. South Africa is the workshop of the region. If there is infrastructure development in Zambia, Malawi and Zimbabwe, many of the products will be sourced in South Africa. It is in the country's best interests to provide outward development finance that supports the major industrial and infrastructure projects in the region.

It could be argued that it is not politically possible to justify investing in infrastructure in another country when South Africa has such great needs. But this is not necessarily an either/or choice. Since the industrial growth in this country is linked to the growth of the region, investment in neighbouring countries will stimulate employment in South Africa and, therefore, the revenue and tax base. Despite its high levels of poverty and unemployment, South Africa is still the 'Germany' of the region. Germany invested in infrastructure throughout southern Italy and Spain because that was where they would sell products. (The investments also, of course, affected migration patterns in the longer term.) South Africa can become the regional hub for competitive intermediate products, capital equipment and consumer durables. It should not be competing with Lesotho in low-cost clothing but should be producing fridges, freezers, durable goods, building products and inputs for infrastructure projects. This is reflected in the new IPAP.

This approach raises two broad policy issues around regional intervention and macroeconomic policy. If the exchange rate stays the same, the country cannot expect a different outcome from its industrial policy. If the exchange rate continues to reflect the carry trade and high interest rates, the country will not succeed in developing competitive tradable sectors. The third policy issue is the financial sector: how is investment in productive, labour-absorbing capacity financed? This points to development finance and to interventions in the financial sector. Even requiring the banks to report their lending by sector would be a huge step forward. Banks are not required to collect the data, whereas banks in Botswana report by manufacturing subsector. Although this may be easier to do in a small economy such as Botswana, it would not be an odious requirement for South African banks to categorise their lending this way.

In summary, the way forward for industrial policy is broadly reflected in IPAP 2. The principal aspects are that an activist industrial policy is central to rapid industrialisation. The government needs to have a deliberate impact on incentive structures so that they reflect future structural change instead of entrenching the old structure. Industrial policy needs to make positive choices to alter the development trajectory, including critically engaging with the strategies of large firms. This must be linked to macroeconomic policy and interventions in the financial sector. Such policies must also be regional in vision.

What are the implications for the state? It needs a centre to analyse industry and firm strategies; this can draw from public institutions such as the IDC or the Competition Commission. It needs to enhance coordination by establishing an institutional core for an industrial strategy, with appropriate tools for implementation. To this end, it must identify critical influences on business, including differential electricity tariffs, transport infrastructure, trade tariffs and finance.

Reference

Commission on Growth and Development, 2008. Overview, *The growth report: Strategies for sustained growth and inclusive development.* Washington: World Bank. www.growthcommission.org/storage/cgdev/documents/Report/growthreportoverview.pdf

5. Financialisation and corporate restructuring of the South African economy

Seeraj Mohamed

South Africa has been undergoing a process of deindustrialisation since the 1980s, when big business shored up apartheid and responded to sanctions, and a structure of diversified conglomerates controlled the economy. After 1994, there was significant corporate restructuring, unbundling and listing offshore and, with that, capital flight. In fact, capital flight after 1994 was bigger than it had been through the 1980s (Mohamed & Finnoff, 2005). South African firms restructured inward and diversified out of the economy, moving away from local manufacturing and staying in the high-rent, easy-profit sectors. Some, such as Anglo American's mining companies, were also involved in *global* corporate restructuring. This long-term process of deindustrialisation remained largely unnoticed and an industrial policy strategy to counter it was only developed in the last year or two.

At the same time, the macroeconomic and financial policy framework permitted uncontrolled capital flows by residents and non-residents into the economy. Large amounts of South African money were allowed to move offshore and the big corporations, like Anglo American, become foreign investors. The capital flight, trade mis-invoicing and transfer pricing that the corporations had been doing before were now done more legally.

South Africa had an unemployment and deindustrialisation crisis before the global financial crisis. These problems were exacerbated by debt-driven consumption and speculation in the financial markets. The economy is increasingly fragile because a large trade deficit, which depends on short-term capital flows, has been allowed to develop. The current crisis merely masks many pre-existing problems, such as structural industrial weaknesses and an increased reliance on mining and minerals following the deindustrialisation process.

The recent pattern of growth in South Africa is similar to the debt-driven consumption-based growth and increased investment in the services sectors that characterised the United States before the recession. South Africa also had speculative asset bubbles in real estate and finance, and increased construction and car sales. Central to these continued weaknesses is the role of the financial sector, which has emulated the behaviour of financial institutions in the United States by increasing leverage and contributing to the misallocation of capital.

In the 1990s there was massive global corporate restructuring, a trend reflected in South Africa. Worldwide mergers, which can be seen as a proxy for the global corporate restructuring, grew from less than US$0,5 trillion to an unprecedented US$3,4 trillion. While there were increases in mergers and acquisitions within national economies in the 1980s, especially in the United States, the scale of the global mergers and acquisitions completely dwarfs that. The global restructuring had two elements: a process of concentrating the global economy and a large-scale intervention by institutional investors in the vanguard of the shareholder value movement. Since the restructuring, non-financial corporations have become much more dependent on finance. There have been significant share buybacks to protect these large corporations from being taken over. Anglo American recently took the same type of rearguard action: it increased debt to buy back shares and increase the share price. This has been happening globally; South Africa is simply following the trend. After 2001, increasing numbers of South African firms moved money offshore, including Anglo American, which became a global mining company.

The engine of South African growth has been short-term capital flows. Between 1990 and 2008 there were only four positive years: 1997, 2001, 2005 and 2007 – and the first two are aberrations caused by the major offshore listings. On paper, these companies became foreign investors in South Africa and their assets became foreign, but South Africa received no new capital. In 2005, 38% of South Africa's largest banking group was sold to Barclays and, in 2007/08, 20% of Standard Bank was sold to ICBC China. The inflow of foreign direct investment was mainly for finance and the odd portfolio investment. Kindleberger (2005) shows that every major financial crisis since the 14th century was preceded by a surge in short-term capital flows. Such inflows shock the macroeconomy and increase debt speculation and consumption, which create bubbles. Eventually the debt cannot be repaid. Money rapidly leaves the economy and a crash follows.

South Africa saw a large increase in short-term flows from 1994 until the currency crash in 2001. Inflows recovered until 2006, peaking at nearly 8% of GDP. When the financial crisis hit, the rand depreciated by more than 30%, even before the large outflows occurred. Portfolio flows have since recovered, as has the rand (by 35%). Such uncontrolled movement of short-term capital drives huge volatility in the macro variables, especially the exchange rate. Net other capital flows were mostly negative until 2005, after which the carry trade increased rapidly as foreigners took advantage of the interest rates to 'park' their money here for very short periods. The carry trade is even more volatile than portfolio flows, and South Africa's balance of payments survived on the carry trade through most of the financial crisis – a particularly fragile position.

These short-term flows bring huge liquidity into the economy. The money flows into the rest of the economy, to the banks. Credit extension to the private sector increased by 22% from 2000 to 2008 but private business investment increased by only 5%. The widely held view that South Africans are not saving is not correct: the money has been going to the private sector, which has seen the kind of leverage that occurred in the United States. The South African financial sector was, in fact, saved by the crisis, because it was going the same way as the banking system in the United States.

By 2007, the South African derivatives market had grown to five times its size in 2004. This reflects the global growth in future contracts. The banks used these derivatives to increase leverage but the money was spent on credit card purchases, cars, mortgages, short-term debt and collaterisation.

Corporations are also misallocating their investments. The Reserve Bank's flow-of-funds data from 1992 to 2007 show that, except in two years, the net acquisition of financial assets by the corporate sector was higher than its fixed investment. Apart from those two years, the corporate sector speculated in the financial markets more than it invested.

This is part of a global trend as well. As economies financialise, the markets have a much shorter perspective and non-financial corporations become increasingly financialised. In very competitive product markets, they are driven to show higher returns and turn to speculation in financial assets to shore up their bottom line. The pattern in South Africa is in line with the global pattern for large corporations.

General Electric is a good example. Having to compete with cheaper assembled products from China and the East, it moved into GE Finance, which eventually became bigger than the productive side of the business. To boost the returns of GE Finance, the company became a serial acquirer of financial firms. It effectively bought the profitability of other firms and sold them off afterwards. This, rather than the notion of 'changing production systems' or 'Six Sigma', is the 'secret' of [former General Electric Chief Executive] Jack Welch. It is about the serial acquisition of finance, financialising the business and thereby killing the productive sector.

This kind of behaviour also happens in South Africa. Of the 27 manufacturing sectors in the economy, 17 had a decrease in capital stock between 2000 and 2008. The economy lost capacity in medium-technology industries and labour-intensive manufacturing, as well as in sectors like agriculture, forestry and fishing, beverages, textiles, printing, footwear and clothing. All of these sectors are now effectively depleted.

Discussion

The discussion focused on the sources of capital in the South African economy, looking at foreign portfolio investment and the often-perverse role of domestic savings.

Fine (2009) suggests that the financial sector and big business supported a slow relaxation of exchange controls in part to maintain the strength of the rand until they needed to convert their rand to a foreign currency. This means the macroeconomic policy framework and finance policies are geared towards helping the big corporations engage in capital flight; the increased financialisation of South African economy is linked to this process. The government and the Reserve Bank created the macroeconomic and financial frameworks in line with the policies of the Washington Consensus, which are geared towards finance, not industry. Part of this crisis reflects the fact that the rentiers have increased their excesses to the point of destroying the productive sectors of the economy. It shows that those strategies have been unviable and must be reversed. Foreign equity investment can help local industry if it is done in a controlled way. When there are 'speed bumps' to slow down the movement of capital and make it less speculative, the amount of available capital may even increase.

However, the South African economy may not need foreign money. Local money has been going to the wrong places. The argument that South Africa saves too little is inappropriate. Savings force down aggregate demand at a time when aggregate demand should be rising, especially among the poorest people. The mentality of generating higher savings also drives up interest rates. The worst part is that the higher the savings, the larger the misallocation of capital because savings are used for financial speculation rather than fixed investment. House prices are recovering so the banks are starting to feel confident again. They are lending money for mortgages, but not to poor people who need houses; rather, the money goes to people who speculate in the housing and real estate markets.

Since 1994, issues about trade and competitiveness within the framework of the World Trade Organization have attracted so much attention that many missed the big picture. Even if South Africa had the cheapest labour and the like, big business was just not interested in staying. Anglo American had hundred-odd subsidiaries in retail and manufacturing but they simply unloaded these subsidiaries.

Households and business are currently dissaving – spending more than what they earn. That process develops *as* a country becomes dependent on short-term capital flows. As firms become more speculative, they start dissaving. They (and households too) become much larger investors in the financial sector and incur increased debt for speculation. This process of opening up to short-term flows and allowing them to become dominant (and create bubbles in the economy) has made short-term foreign inflows the major source of savings.

South Africa has allowed banks to develop a shadow banking system. There is much discussion about industrial policy and changing the growth path but too little about the role of finance within these processes. There are many short-term measures to use but, in the longer term, an understanding of the decision-making of banks and large firms is crucial. The conditions that banks set in their contracts are a powerful influence on industry.

The first option is to make better use of state institutions. The second is to reconsider the way banks are governed, whether through the Reserve Bank or regulation. There is a continuum within the experience of developing countries, from the dictatorial, like South Korea, which takes control of the financial sector, to a country like Brazil, where the state drives industrial finance and provides concessional finance to industry. South Africa needs to look at this range of experience and find aspects that fit local conditions.

In this seminar series, the agenda must be carefully focused around what the government can do and why it does not do it. Is it reasonable to ask the government to do more or different things to affect the structure of the economy? This is the subject of the last session.

References

Fine, B, 2009. Political economy for the rainbow nation: Dividing the spectrum? *Making sense of borders: Identity, citizenship and power in South Africa*, South African Sociological Association Annual Conference, 28 June–2 July, Johannesburg. eprints.soas.ac.uk/7972/1/sasa_benfine.pdf

Kindleberger, C & Aliber, R, 2005. *Manias, panics and crashes: A history of financial crises*. New Jersey: John Wiley and Sons.

Mohamed, S & Finnoff, K, 2005. Capital flight from South Africa, 1980–2000. In: Epstein, G (ed.) *Capital flight and capital controls in developing countries*. Cheltenham, UK and Northampton, MA: Edward Elgar Publishing.

6. The mining value chain

Richard Goode

This presentation looks backwards at the way the economy has been constructed around minerals and forward to some of the possibilities for further value creation.

Mining created South Africa's modern industrial economy but it has a brutal and ugly past with extremely vicious exploitation. Mining is dominant because of the unusual richness of South Africa's mineral resources. There are two great geological complexes: the Gold Fields on the Witwatersrand and the Igneous (platinum nickel) Complex in the Bushveld. These fields gave South Africa a long mining history and will continue to do so. Although mining still has much to contribute, it is a mature industry. South Africa does not have the enormous untapped potential of other developing countries, many of which are in Africa. Most of the obvious opportunities for value creation from South Africa's mineral sector have already been exploited. In this process, mining was a determinant of the economic trajectory of the country.

South Africa still possesses important critical mineral reserves. For example, it has the world's largest reserves of chrome. It still has the largest reserves of gold, although its status as a gold producer has slipped into third place behind China and the United States, with Australia not far behind. This reflects the maturity of the industry. The development of underground mining to exploit these mineral riches required considerable technical ingenuity but much of this technical capability has little application outside the country. South Africa is not at the cutting edge of mining or extractive technology.

Mineral products contribute about 8% to GDP, with an investment contribution that is slightly ahead of its share of GDP, at 9%. It contributes significantly (33%) to export earnings. The industry employs 2,5% of the economically active population but provides only 0,5% of state revenue.

What is the real contribution of the mining industry? It is the critical sector underpinning South Africa's exports, but this continues its historical trajectory as an extractive industry most noted for its exports. Over time, mining's share in the economy has shrunk, despite the exaggerated spike caused by the high price of gold in 1980. The mining sector did grow considerably during the last cycle of the commodities boom but mining production and exports declined rapidly after mid-2008.

The traditional minerals value chain has four stages. The first stage is extraction and the second primary processing. After extraction, where mining ends, there is an overlap with primary processing – the production of a first-stage beneficiated product. From then on, mining products go into manufacturing (stage 3) and finished manufactures (stage 4), which are quite far removed from mining.

Chemicals, energy and minerals dominate the manufacturing sector, contributing over 40% of manufacturing GDP. 'Minerals and energy complex' is a valid phrase that demonstrates the significance of the mineral sector and its heavily interlinked energy component. It is a consequence of South Africa's resource endowment but has also strongly shaped the development path of the country.

Table 6.1 shows that South Africa does most of the easy beneficiation that is appropriate for its balance of resources and the corresponding minerals. Using gold as an example, South Africa has a comparative advantage in processing gold ores. It

Table 6.1: Beneficiation of mining products in South Africa

Commodity	Stage 1 Ores and concentrates (%)	Stage 2 Processed and refined ore (%)	Stage 3 Primary manufacture (%)	Stage 4 Finished manufacture (%)
Gold	100	100	5	2
Diamonds	100	100	6	–
Platinum group metals	100	100	–	6
Iron ore to steel	100	30	30	15
Chrome to stainless steel	100	85	9	3
Coal	100	65	–	65
Aluminium	0	100	30	11
Zinc	100	100	90	60
Manganese	100	50	25	22
Titanium	100	15	4	Small
Copper	100	100	65	50
Scrap	–	–	50	70

does very little of the finished manufacture – South Africa is not a good producer of jewellery, and the markets that offer a greater opportunity for beneficiation are not necessarily the jewellery markets. South Africa's competitive advantage is in the production of gold. Gold that is available at exactly the same price in Johannesburg as it is in Mumbai means that there is no price advantage for a jeweller in South Africa to design and transform that material. The factors that have a bigger influence on successful jewellery production are design innovation, the cost of labour and the marketing channels. Those are poorly developed in South Africa. That said, South Africa has lost considerable ground in the manufacture of gold, platinum and diamond jewellery, and there may well be room to catch up.

In the table, the relatively high values for the processing of coal show that there may not be many opportunities for further processing of this mineral. South Africa needs to focus on finding applications where it has the ability to dominate the subsequent processing of the material and not simply be the producer that unloads a surplus on the world market.

This classic view of the minerals commodity chain – from extraction to processing, manufacturing to recycling, and the limits to further processing – has encouraged South Africa to look at other economies that have successfully used their resource endowment to industrialise. The United States, Australia and the Scandinavian countries are not examples for South Africa to emulate but they provide useful lessons. Successful processing requires a combination of goods and services. The supply industries create the linkages that, in turn, foster the dynamism and clustered activities that are the expressions of competitive industries and sources of innovation.

Mining-related activities have both low- and high-tech aspects. There are major inputs for services, equipment and the development of unique processes where off-the-shelf solutions or generic equipment are combined to suit a particular requirement. Some of these items may become commodified but, as every plant has to be purposely designed and constructed, there is protection against being displaced by the commodified manufactured goods that are critical inputs into the mining sector. For this reason, an alternative view of the minerals value chain is advocated, which consciously seeks to identify the opportunities created by the business of mining, processing and distributing mineral products. Figure 6.1 highlights four important activities. Downstream value addition (1) is by no means closed off to further development in South Africa but most of the easy opportunities have long been exploited. Increasing attention should be given to side-stream opportunities (2) that are created by demand from

Figure 6.1: Mining sector linkages

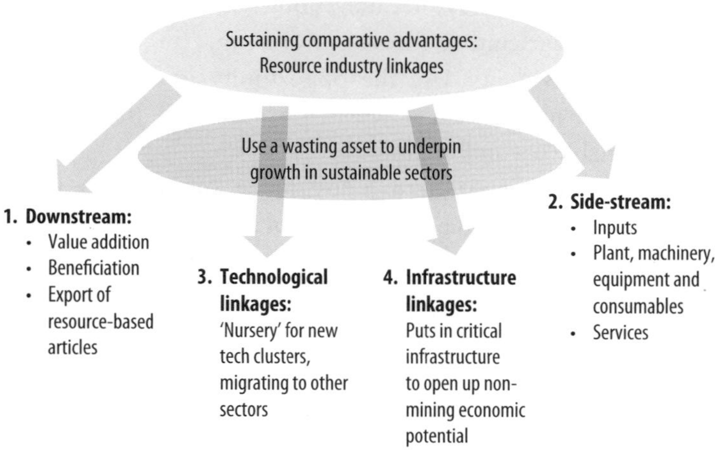

Sustaining comparative advantages: Resource industry linkages

Use a wasting asset to underpin growth in sustainable sectors

1. **Downstream:**
   - Value addition
   - Beneficiation
   - Export of resource-based articles

2. **Side-stream:**
   - Inputs
   - Plant, machinery, equipment and consumables
   - Services

3. **Technological linkages:** 'Nursery' for new tech clusters, migrating to other sectors

4. **Infrastructure linkages:** Puts in critical infrastructure to open up non-mining economic potential

the minerals industry and where South Africa has competitive advantages. From a developmental point of view, an important area concerns technical and infrastructural linkages (3 & 4). For example, the development of coal exports through Richards Bay created the impetus for its development as a major deep-water port, which in turn stimulated significant manufacturing activity in northern KwaZulu-Natal. Similar opportunities are created where the necessary investment for exploiting a mineral resource can trigger other activity in agriculture and services.

The mindset of 'mining for development' specifically looks at the various economic activities generated by mining and the problems and opportunities of each activity. These include the following:

- *Mineral rents:* Invest in physical and social infrastructure for future growth and development, which is sustainable beyond mining. Even a consensus-seeking initiative like the KwaZulu-Natal Growth Coalition, which represents conventional views, recognises the importance of mineral rents and the possibility of creating a fund for development beyond mining.

- *Mineral infrastructure:* Use mineral infrastructure (e.g. transport and energy) to catalyse other sustainable potential, such as in agriculture, forestry or tourism.
- *Mineral feedstocks:* Use the opportunity of available raw materials to establish downstream industries that will be sustainable beyond mining.
- *Mining market:* Establish industries to supply the mining industry, which will be sustainable beyond mining.
- *Technical migration*: Invest in research and development for technological challenges that could migrate into other sectors and be sustainable beyond mining.

Ideally, minerals development can be conceptualised as per Figure 6.2. However, success in each of these stages depends on activities outside the mining industry, largely in manufacturing. Success also depends on the general requirements of resource-based development, such as infrastructure, human resources, skills and innovation systems. Without these, the 'enclave' character of mining will be left unaltered.

What is the way forward? In a crude generalisation, the processing of outputs from mines represents a price differential of 10% to 15%. This means that the competitiveness of downstream industries is not utterly dependent on the efficiency in the mining sector: the conversion efficiency is also important. Barriers that continue to determine firm behaviour include import parity pricing, the nature of the South African market, its position in regional and global markets, and the terms of trade on which South Africa engages with the rest of the world.

South African firms have a significant presence in regional markets. They provide solutions to the domestic market and have fairly large and successful export activities. However, South Africa's mining sector is by no means able to dominate. It faces a number of constraints, the most important of which may well be the lack of financing packages to support the

Figure 6.2: Matrix of resource-based development

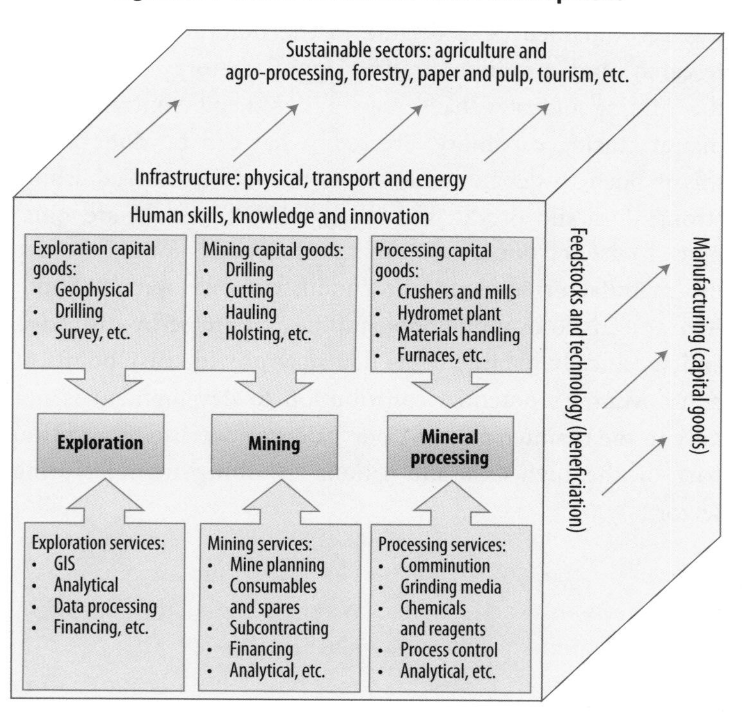

procurement of South African equipment for mineral projects in the region.

Where in the mining value chain do locally domiciled transnational corporations and local firms have a significant presence? The mining industry is a globalised specification market. The requirements for a particular piece of equipment are not based on brand characteristics but on technical specifications. Transnational companies that operate in South Africa supply the specialist needs of the local industry from production bases elsewhere in the world. South Africa should use the opportunity to build on the progress that its firms have already made and provide significant support and intervention to preserve their competitiveness.

The offshoring of South Africa's major mining companies was accompanied by a decline in the domestic capacity for research and production. The input sectors that service the mining industry have seen a significant contraction of manufacturing capability. Precisely what can be done about this is open to debate, because the barriers to re-establishing strong domestic production in a globalised world are quite high. To use the opportunity that mining offers for an effective pro-manufacturing platform for industrial development, South Africa needs to examine opportunities on a case-by-case basis and specifically identify areas that may provide easy points of entry. Mining's potential contribution to development is not only in the maintenance of trade balances but also as a critical part of the high-tech and labour-absorbing manufacturing sector.

7. Driving value addition in the South African economy

Nimrod Zalk

Peter Nolan shows that the so-called 'global business revolution' – the global corporate restructuring since the 1990s – resulted in significantly higher levels of concentration in long value chains, which are generally controlled by companies of the North. William Milberg at the New School for Social Research in New York studied the role of power as part of value chain analysis. He shows that, despite the industrial decline in the United States, its financial system still manages to draw increasing shares of the global value added because it controls the (American) corporations at the top of the global value chains. This creates a concentrated global structure where the surpluses have been drawn out: companies in the United States and Europe control the engineering, design, branding and distribution, and they are beholden to the financial system to show increasing returns. They are pressuring mining countries like South Africa and assembling countries like China to get larger returns. Part of the process of financialisation is linked to this increased control and pressuring of global value chains, as is the process of global corporate restructuring. From this perspective, it is clear that South Africa has become more dependent on exports because this fits the objectives of these large corporations.

Returning quickly to the financialisation in the economy discussed earlier, note a couple of linkages. The growth in the financial sector through high levels of credit extension has stimulated the wholesale and retail sector. Trade liberalisation also contributed to the development of a large retail sector that is out of proportion to the size of the economy and its stage of development. The retail sector is fundamentally driven by derived demand.

In the late 1970s rates of saving and investment in South Africa were very high, even with a financial sector that measured only 4% to 5% of GDP. Following a time of moderate growth, the financial sector has shown explosive growth since 1994, more than doubling its share to 13% of GDP. Basic economics teaches that the role of the financial sector is to aggregate savings and put those savings into productive investments. That is not happening. Instead, it can be argued that there has been a massive process of rent extraction from the productive sectors of the economy.

Most of the growth in the financial sector has not manifested itself in fixed investment. Instead, it has gone into a massive extension of credit. What fixed investment did occur was concentrated in finance and insurance, business and other services, and then in the traditional heavy industry and mining sectors.

Dani Rodrik's findings on the profitability of manufacturing relative to the so-called 'FIRE' sector (finance, insurance and real estate) shows a substantial period of declining relative profitability from the early 1990s. This raised the threshold for what is considered a 'suitable' rate of return on an investment in the real economy. The higher threshold has many perverse consequences; for example, it attracts investment into less productive activities.

Industrial policy work shows that manufacturing and high-value secondary sectors are the engine of growth of the economy, although high-value primary and services activity also plays a role. Three arguments support this view. First, manufacturing has traditionally been seen, for example by Lewis (1954), as the engine of industrial development. It allows for the transfer of labour of those who are unemployed or underemployed in the 'traditional' sectors (e.g. subsistence agriculture) to modern sectors, such as manufacturing. It also raises productivity in both sectors.

Second, manufacturing is the main sector to provide the scope for upgrading productivity and income, as argued by Ha-Joon Chang and Sanjaya Lall. It is possible to get economies of scale and increasing returns in manufacturing. Compare this (crudely) to a services activity: a barber can only cut the hair of a limited number of people per day but manufacturing can be scaled up and has many interlocking effects.

The third argument is based on trade: in the long run, there is increasing income elasticity from the demand for manufactured products versus primary products. And, finally, there is scope for a dynamic increase in returns to scale, both at the level of the manufacturing firm and within its cluster or value chain. Such an increase can come from the firm's own efforts to grow or become more efficient and, as more complex industrial clusters develop, from a cluster-wide productivity effect involving increasing specialisation and interaction among the firms in the cluster.

Coming to the sectors that might drive high value-added dynamic increasing returns, the first group comprises those with intermediate barriers to entry, neither too low nor too high. Where barriers to entry are very low (e.g. basic clothing), countries like China and Bangladesh will continue to dominate, for a variety of reasons. This does not mean that South Africa should not produce clothing. It should, but it should also move into areas where it has advantages such as proximity to retailers, or it can use materials that are more sophisticated, or firms can adopt world-class manufacturing practices. The revised Industrial Policy Action Plan (IPAP 2) identifies such sectors.

The second group is a range of sectors where there is complementarity between investment and employment. Investment in equipment does not always mean that labour will be displaced. In some sectors, higher investment leads to higher employment; capital equipment, metal fabrication and plastics fabrication are examples of such sectors.

The third group is sectors with a strong potential for clustering – and therefore dynamic productivity effects – both within and among sectors. These include medium-technology sectors like metals and automotives, which have a strong possibility of building intersectoral linkages.

The last group is downstream beneficiation, which is a contested area. Some argue that it is not useful to conceptualise industrial development through the lens of this pipeline of activity going from, say, iron ore to steel to metal products, and so forth. Ricardo Hausmann from Harvard made this argument. Their econometric look at productive structures across economies showed that the underlying resource base is not related to what is actually produced. There are two extremes to the debate. One side says that this is not a useful concept; the other says that it is necessary.

Whether downstream beneficiation absorbs labour depends on the sector and the value chain; the approach has to be sophisticated. It cannot be argued, across the board, that every single mineral mined in South Africa needs beneficiation. Given the country's energy crisis, this path does not make sense because beneficiation is a capital- and energy-intensive process.

In summary, the IPAP 2 argues that the following sectors may have the potential to drive high value-added dynamic increasing returns:

- *Metal fabrication, capital equipment and transport equipment*: These sectors must be linked to the infrastructure development programme over the next few years. They must first be localised and resuscitated, and then positioned as future exporters.

- *Plastics fabrication:* In this sector, more investment creates more employment.
- *Automotives:* There is a shift in emphasis to deepening the supply of components to automotive assemblers. The various tiers of component supply, both domestic and international, are where value is added and jobs created.
- *Interlinkages* between these areas: Plastics, for instance, requires a demand-pull, for example through fabricated plastics being used in the automotive sector or for packaging.

Before these sectors can succeed, certain underlying capabilities have to be resuscitated. These include tooling, foundries, and the ability to make machine tools and various moulds.

South Africa can also move into the area of medium and heavy commercial vehicles. This relates back to public procurement. In rolling out their bus rapid transport systems, the metropolitan municipalities procure buses from Brazil. Bus assembly is very labour-intensive, and developing this capacity in South Africa could allow for more diversification within the component sector. Next in this range of activities would be the 'yellow metals', such as large articulated dump trucks. Developing all of these capabilities has the potential to generate positive interlocking effects.

The next area has been a big omission from industrial policy: agro-processing. South Africa can move into high-value activities like essential oils, organics, aquaculture and mariculture. Another area is high-value services, like software development. Green industries and technologies could also form an increasing part of manufacturing development, from solar panels and water heating to industrial-size concentrated solar thermal plants.

South Africa can also upgrade areas like furniture or clothing by moving within sectors to more sophisticated activities that add higher value and are less directly in competition with the low-wage countries. In consumer durables, such as fridges and stoves, should the country not be looking to become the major supplier to the subregion?

In summary, the approach is not 'manufacturing fundamentalist'; instead, it looks for economic activities that have desirable characteristics and aims to match and stimulate them across different sectors.

The next issue concerns the levers and instruments to shift relative economic incentives in favour of productive activities. The first, of course, is macroeconomic policy, which is critical. Without shifting the policy to become more favourable to productive activity, development will be much more difficult. The second is procurement linked to localisation. Proposals have been submitted to the Treasury to change the Preferential Procurement Regulations toward local production. In the 10 out of 100 preference points allocated to non-price-based factors, local production and BEE have to loom large. One proposal is that, when a local company does not win a tender because of the price offered by the foreign company, it be given the option of matching the foreign bid. There is also a provision to designate, for certain tenders and industries, that a specific proportion must be manufactured locally.

The third set of tools includes a revision of the National Industrial Participation Programme (NIPP), an offset programme, to make it more strategic. One example would be the purchase of submarines. Once the contract has been awarded, the country's bargaining power to obtain meaningful and strong industrial commitments is limited. The aim is to make offset requirements a more upfront, pre-tender process, so that the industrial and localisation requirements are identified in the tender. This will only apply to specific strategic cases.

Turning to mining, the aim is to ensure that, when the local mining industry invests – whether in South Africa or elsewhere – they use South African mining equipment, manufacturers and suppliers. Part of this concerns the minerals and mining regime; the other concerns how development finance institutions attach conditionalities to funding mining projects in South Africa or the rest of the continent.

In the automotive sector, the intention is to use the Automotive Production and Development Programme, the revised MIDP for much stronger localisation of components, for example, together with higher economies of scale on the assembly side. In this scenario, industrial financing is crucial.

Once these three are in place, they will form a powerful set of instruments to transform the industrialisation and growth path of the South African economy.

There are several issues around finance. There has to be stronger regulation of the financial sector, away from damaging speculative activities. The other side of the equation is that South Africa must be able to control more sources of finance and direct them to the productive sectors of the economy, in particular manufacturing and the sectors identified in the industrial policy.

Brazil is an example of active development finance. By disbursements, Banco Nacional de Desenvolvimento Econômico e Social (BNDES) is the biggest development bank in the world, bigger than the World Bank. (This does not apply to capitalisation: they are more leveraged than the World Bank.) BNDES is financed primarily through the Workers' Assistance Fund (known as the FAT), which is roughly equivalent to South Africa's Workers Compensation Fund and is funded through a payroll tax. About 40% of the Fund is ring-fenced specifically for BNDES to invest. The logic is that Brazil does not want only a defensive strategy for unemployment, providing for people when they are unemployed. It wants to deploy these funds in a proactive pro-employment strategy. BNDES is not required to pay back the capital, only the interest, which makes this a highly concessional source of funding. In addition, BNDES can purchase treasury bonds at an attractive rate.

In practice, BNDES structures its investment by taking the long-term interest rate (about 6,25% last year), adding a basic spread (just over 1% on average) and a credit risk of approximately 1%. This gives an average lending rate of 8,34%, as shown in Table 7.1. The real interest rate in Brazil is 8,08%, which means the real interest rate of BNDES loans is 0,26% (or about half the prime rate).

BNDES finances almost all the industrial and infrastructural investment in Brazil. It has a huge share of credit and investment in the national economy and all of this is channelled to productive investment, not speculative activities. Leading up to the crisis in 2008, the growth of investment in Brazil was 2,5% higher than GDP growth.

South Africa needs such an instrument, without slavishly emulating Brazil, Korea or any other country. There has to be a large source of concessional financing that is channelled towards the real economy. One way to mobilise this kind of financing (and this also goes to the downstream beneficiation debate) is to ring-fence the royalties that mining companies are obliged to pay and put them in a downstream investment fund, administered – this is the Treasury's preference – by the IDC. Everybody, except half of the International Monetary Fund, agrees that taxing mining companies is an appropriate response. Mining resources will not last forever.

Another possibility to explore is the Unemployment Insurance Fund. It has about R23 billion in surplus funds that are currently managed by the PIC on the same basis that it manages the Government Employees Pension Fund. This is not the most productive use of these funds. Note that there is a difference between the two funds. Due to their nature, pension funds should be invested more conservatively; there is no suggestion of using the Government Employees Pension Fund for industrial development.

Table 7.1: Comparison of the IDC and BNDES

Indicators	IDC, South Africa	BNDES, Brazil
Source of loan financing	• Commercial bank loans • Loans from commercial development finance institutions	• Workers' Assistance Fund (FAT) – Legislatively mandated flow of large portion of FAT (+40%) – BNDES repays only interest, not capital • Treasury bonds on attractive terms
Structure of loan financing		
Long-term interest rate	8,8%	6,25% (TJLP)
Basic spread	1%	0% to 3% (average approx. 1,09%)
Credit risk levy	0% to 4%	0,46% to 3,57%
Average credit risk levy (approximate)	1,7%	1%
Real interest rate of loans		
Average lending rate	11,5%	8,34%
Real bank rate	4,92%	7,61%
Real interest rate	6,58%	0,73%

Further to the use of localisation and regionalisation as conditionalities of project finance, when the Development Bank of Southern Africa (DBSA) or IDC invests in a large project, how does this bring along South African suppliers? When they invest in projects outside South Africa, whether in Botswana or the Congo, how can a greater premium be put on sourcing local inputs and building industrial capacity there?

Another important source of funding is global money that is available for green industries. The conditionalities attached must be treated with care but it is certainly a potential source of funding for green energy, including solar and wind generation, biomass and recycling.

In trade policy, there is scope for a strategic and selective increase in tariffs within the bound rates on products that have a significant potential for employment or import replacement. A second option is to review standards to lock out unsafe and low-quality imports and lock in access to export markets; this will be important for the agri-processing area. How can these be oriented more strategically? Third is the judicious use of export taxes, while taking into account various factors like future investment behaviour. For example, the government is contemplating a tax on the export of scrap.

There are two areas of focus in the efforts around competition policy. The first is to drive down the cost of inputs into manufacturing and other productive processes, like steel, chemicals and fertilisers. The second is to reduce the price of wage goods and other products purchased largely by poor and working-class households, such as food.

Another task is to revisit BEE so that expansionary BEE transactions in productive sectors receive higher recognition and support than straightforward transfers of ownership. Maybe the codes should be revisited to link BEE more closely to localisation. A related point, which was a huge weakness of the transition, is the failure to create a significant black manufacturing class in South Africa. (There are reasons for this: the transactions have primarily followed high economic rents and sectors that can absorb such large transactions.) Without a black manufacturing class, there will not be sufficient voice for the kind of policies that promote the productive sectors of the economy.

The Department of Mineral Resources is apparently considering a review of mining legislation and policy. This is an opportunity to strengthen the requirements for downstream and side-stream beneficiation. (Downstream means further processing along the value chain; side-stream is largely the provision of capital goods and services into the mining sector itself.)

In skills development, a much stronger alignment is needed between sector strategies, Sector Education and Training Authorities (SETAs) and skills plans. From a sector development perspective, this was done quite well in two sectors, clothing and business processes, asking what skills are required and making active inputs into the process. This could become a model for the dti to work more proactively in the services strategy. A related area, which is often overlooked, is the presence of highly developed skills infrastructure within the geographic space and using the same machinery as the industry, such as training centres for metal fabrication or the clothing industry. The government should look at resuscitating this infrastructure; it will not happen through the private sector or through the weak signals of the skills system. It requires more focused investment.

Other activities are not being pursued because the enabling legislation and regulation are not in place. Biofuels is one example: it needs a mandatory uplift of biofuels into the broader fuel supply. The fuel companies will not voluntarily purchase biofuels and must be obliged to buy a certain percentage at a particular price. Aquaculture and mariculture – fish farming – need complex regulation. Green industries require the extension of the renewable energy feed-in tariffs (REFITs), more sources of energy supply and a higher threshold within the energy mix. As electricity prices rise, industrial energy efficiency will become more important and require a set of interventions.

The government has certain areas of focus for beneficiation. First, in downstream beneficiation, it sees metal processing as important, for instance for transport equipment. A critical concern along this value chain is the practice of import parity pricing. It does not derive from the mining side of the activity but rather from the market power of the intermediate processing side.

Other downstream activities could include processing polymers into plastics; gold and platinum into jewellery;

and platinum group metals into catalytic converters, diesel particulate filters and the other requirements of the emerging hydrogen economy. This is where the global growth seems to occur. Should South Africa levy export taxes on platinum? Only a small proportion of the platinum output is used for such activities. Another approach would be to levy a higher royalty on platinum and direct those funds to downstream activities, rather than try to force the beneficiation of particular commodities. The government is also looking at mining as a source of demand for manufacturing – capital equipment and other inputs – not just for South Africa but also for the rest of the world.

On the upstream side, with South Africa's energy shortages and increased costs, it must be strategic about the activities, like smelting or refining, that it can support. The government is looking at increasing competition in the steel sector. New technologies make for interesting possibilities, such as building mini-mills rather than huge integrated mills. Another option is products that feed into high-value downstream value chains; for instance, titanium and rhodium can feed into the solar, nuclear and aerospace value chains. The conditionalities must be set in advance: instead of supporting the upstream in the hope that the downstream will come, stipulate that support for a project means that a preferential price will be set for outputs offered to downstream firms.

There is a debate within the administration about why industrial development needs support rather than education, health and housing. It is a legitimate question. There are many reasons. Many sub-Saharan African countries achieved impressive results in education and health, such as Zimbabwe in the decades just after independence. However, if South Africa does not pay sufficient attention to the productive side of the economy, high unemployment, also among graduates, will remain. Also, even if social spending is a large proportion of GDP, the spending will always be limited by the size of the GDP itself.

Then there is the question of the efficiency of spending: is South Africa not already spending enough on health or education? What is the scope for increasing the efficiency and effectiveness of that spending? Lastly, industrial support is not a zero-sum game. Owing to its strong linkages and multipliers, support for industrial development stimulates growth and job creation, improves the trade balance and increases net tax revenue.

References

Economic Sectors and Employment Cluster, 2010. *2010/11 – 2012/13 Industrial Policy Action Plan* [IPAP]. www.info.gov.za/view/DownloadFileAction?id=117330

Lewis, WA, 1954. Economic development with unlimited supplies of labour. *Manchester School of Economic and Social Studies*, 22: 139–91.

Rodrik, D, 2006. *Understanding South Africa's economic puzzles.* Cambridge: Harvard University Center for International Development, p. 51. www.nber.org/papers/12565.pdf

8. Value-added chain

Nnzeni Netshitomboni

In its most basic form, the value-added chain is the process by which technology is combined with material and labour inputs, and these process inputs are assembled, marketed and distributed. This suggests a linear sequence of the operations needed to produce and distribute goods and services. However, global production networks are considerably more complex, both organisationally and geographically.

Knowing how global value chains operate is essential to understanding how developing countries can access world markets. Access to the markets of developed countries increasingly depends on participation in the global production networks of firms that are based in these countries. The globalisation of trade and production is one of the principal features of the world economy, where transnational corporations are now clearly dominant. The role of these corporations affects not only the fortunes of firms and the structure of industries but also, importantly, how and why developing countries advance, or fail to advance, in the global economy.

Consumption has become the driving force of production, as evidenced by, for example, the branded retail products that are manufactured and used all over the world. Global firms, and particularly transnational corporations, increasingly focus on their core competencies and outsource their non-core manufacturing activities both domestically and abroad. Therefore, production is now more fragmented across nations and geographic space, and trade more integrated. While the growth of world GDP has been strong, world export volumes have grown exponentially. Since production has been broken down into components and intermediate goods, products now cross borders on a regular basis.

Note that the trade figures show the movement of goods across borders while the GDP figures only show value added. Suppose a casing is imported from Thailand into Japan to make a watch; it is recorded in the trade data when it crosses into Japan from Thailand. Once the watch has been assembled and is ready for export to the United States, the full value of the product is again recorded in the trade figures. In contrast, GDP figures measure only the value addition in Japan.

Globally, about 40% of exports are intermediate goods. In Taiwan, the proportion is about 70%, because the country focuses on electronics manufacturing, which involves large-scale exports of intermediate goods and components.

Figure 8.1 depicts a typical linear value chain of the South African agriculture sector. It shows that 47% of the 46 000 commercial farmers are involved in livestock production and

Figure 8.1: Agricultural value chain

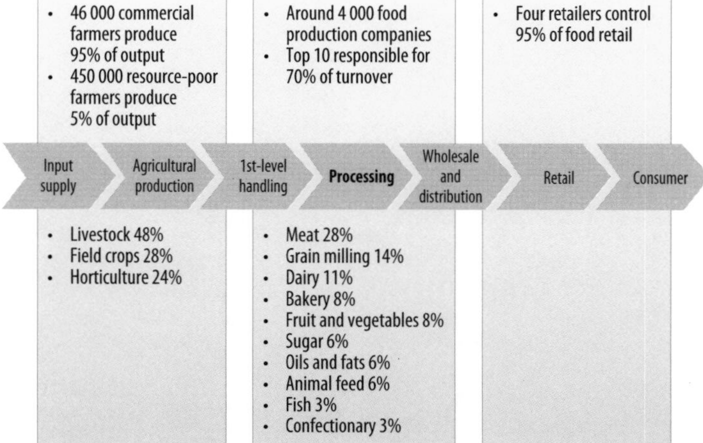

24% in horticulture. South Africa imports significant volumes of wheat and rubber products, and exports citrus and grapes. As for the export of processed agricultural products, these are mainly wine and vegetable products. It is important to remember the vital role of the natural environment, as all production depends on it.

In summary, value chain analysis helps to illuminate South Africa's path to sustainable economic development. The role of transnational corporations remains central to the global economy. Also, where intermediate goods form a large share of trade between nations, this reflects the growing fragmentation of production and the integration of trade. A closer analysis of national and regional value chains will provide a clearer picture.

9. The South African agro-food regime

Ben Cousins

This presentation reflects the work of the Institute for Poverty, Land and Agrarian Studies (PLAAS) on the South African 'agro-food regime'. While there is information about concentration in food retail or milling and storage, there is very little information on the sector as a whole and constructing a picture of the agro-food regime has not been easy.

There are two ways of understanding the sector. The narrower way examines value (or commodity) chains, which link agents and functions in the production of a commodity in all its stages, including the consumption of the final product. The original purpose of this well-known concept was to analyse price formation and the distribution of value. The notion of an agro-food regime is broader. In addition to value chains, it examines social relations and institutions in the markets for food, which are characterised by unequal power relations between agents. This is a political economy view rather than a neoclassical view. Markets are viewed as being imbued with politics rather than distorted by politics. This analysis distinguishes between state regulation via legislation, policy and administrative measures (which neoclassical economists see as market 'distortions') and private regulation within markets, which comprises different forms of power and control.

Understanding value chains in a narrow sense is important; price formation and distribution of value *are* crucial. However, this needs to be embedded in a broader understanding of how power and control can structure markets. This approach is particularly important when there are high levels of concentration at any particular point in a value chain or (and often simultaneously) high levels of vertical concentration. Power and control are vital for understanding these issues.

Note that agriculture is not just about farming; it includes all the linkages from farms, whether backwards (upstream) or forwards (downstream). Since World War II, corporate agribusiness has played an increasingly critical role globally, upstream and downstream; this is analysed in detail in the literature on the food regime.

Farming, however, is still a central component of agriculture. It depends on biological or organic properties, as do diet and health at the consumption end. It is highly unrealistic to consider removing farming from nature into factories with hydroponics, soil, chemicals and artificial light. This could only happen in a small number of highly specialised cases, since it is incredibly expensive and requires significant use of fossil fuels. Agriculture will remain highly dependent on natural cycles of organic matter, nutrients, water and so on. Also, land is a primary productive asset and its distribution remains at issue in South Africa and many parts of the world.

Farming is embedded within complex market structures in wider circuits of capital, which are increasingly transnational. Agriculture in South Africa is integrated into the global agro-food regime and changes in the sector need to be assessed against the backdrop of international changes.

Figure 9.1 is a preliminary sketch of value chains in South Africa's agro-food regime. While farm production is important, inputs to agriculture, wholesale markets, retail markets, processing and packaging, supply to wholesale markets and consumption all play vital roles. For instance, the manipulation of consumption is an important part of the emerging global

Figure 9.1: Value chains within South Africa's agro-food regime

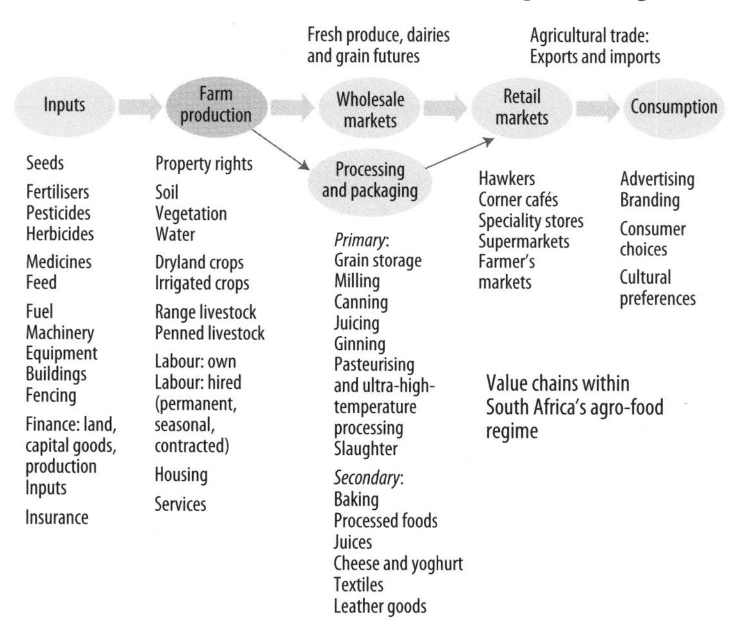

agro-food regime. Agriculture consists of a large number of individual value chains for different products. This system is too complex to map in its entirety and the abstract model in the diagram shows the primary inputs, from seeds to insurance.

Property rights are a crucial factor in farming, as are soil, water and vegetation. Dryland and irrigated crops have different effects on the value chain. Since dryland crops often provide inputs for animal feed, this subsector has an additional linkage within the agricultural sector. The same holds for ranged and penned livestock. Globally, meat is produced from intensely factory-farmed and penned livestock that are grown incredibly fast. This displaces the practice of keeping animals on a natural range. There are important consequences to factory farming, including in South Africa. Labour input is also important, whether the farmer's own or hired labour. The employment dimension is critical: South Africa has seen dramatic losses in agricultural employment over the last decade or two.

As for the other elements of the diagram, processing and packaging relate to the food-based manufactured products sold in supermarkets; these are highly diverse and complicated processes. Wholesale markets remain important, in particular for fresh and dairy produce; they also include the speculative futures market. In retail markets, it is important to understand the so-called 'supermarket revolution', both in South Africa and internationally. The way that food is retailed and consumed is changing fundamentally with the rise of fast foods, the importance of international brands, and the manipulation of consumption by large actors in the value chain.

Figure 9.2 shows the range of agro-processing in South Africa. It is taken from a report called *Re-governing markets* (Vorley et al, 2007), which analysed the value chain in international agriculture. In this diagram, the input side – fertilisers, seeds or chemicals – is missing. The project only considered the downstream aspects of agriculture and ignored the powerful upstream players in the agro-food regime, which shape both production and consumption.

Turning to farm production, the land claims process will transfer commercial farms to previously dispossessed people in the next year or so. The question arises whether the transferred land will still be used for large-scale commercial farming.

Consider the history of farming in South Africa. Agriculture has declined from 21% of GDP in 1911 to only 4% in 1999. However, it remains an important part of the economy, accounting for about 10% of employment and 6% of exports. The value of its backward and forward linkages has been put at 20% to 30% of the economy.

In 1994, the new government inherited a very dualistic and racialised agrarian economy, with about 60 000 large-scale commercial farmers, almost all of whom were white. Only about

Figure 9.2: Agro-processing in South Africa

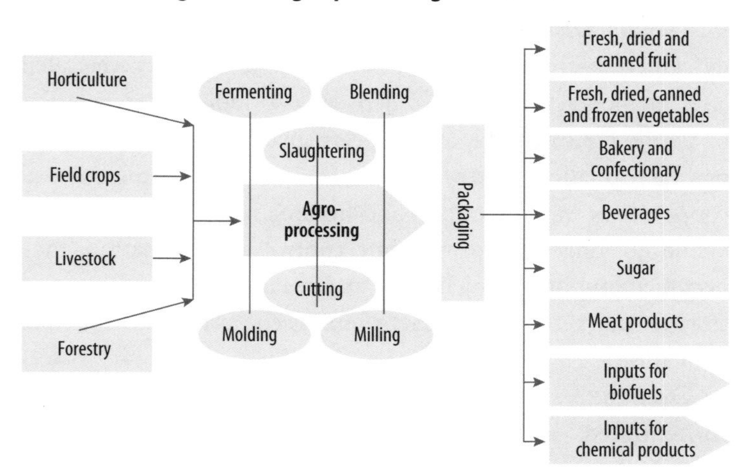

45 000 of them remain, on 86% of agricultural land. The other 14% of land is used by roughly 2 million so-called 'subsistence' farmers and maybe 200 000 semi-commercial smallholders. There is nothing in between: the sector is highly dualistic.

From the 1930s onwards, the commercial farming sector received massive state support through controlled input and output prices, single-channel marketing boards, subsidised credit and drought relief. This meant the income of commercial farmers was all but guaranteed. There were both political and economic reasons for this government support. When mining and industry started to develop, they needed a secure supply of labour. One way to achieve this was to force the rural population into overcrowded homelands where they had no choice but to sell their labour. The political pay-off was that the state then needed to support white agriculture to supply food to society; this generated political support from its constituency. The growth of large-scale commercial farming thus has to be seen as a crucial part of South Africa's history. It played an integral role in the creation of a particular kind of economy.

By the 1980s, however, the extent of state support to this sector was no longer affordable. The liberalisation and deregulation processes that started at that time were accelerated after democracy. In 1996, there was a radical deregulation of public controls and, as has been speculated, an increase in private regulation. One symptom of this was that farmer-owned cooperatives were privatised and became very large businesses. While no longer subject to state control and regulation, they occupied important niches, in particular in the milling and storage markets, and perhaps exercised a form of private regulation.

Over the last 19 years, the sector has become increasingly concentrated, as 'inefficient' large-scale commercial farmers (who had depended on state subsidisation) left agriculture. It has been claimed that this has improved efficiency in the sector.

The composition of the sector also changed: in 1995, 48% of its total value was in field crops. By 2000, this had decreased to 32%. Animal production increased from 36% to 42% in the same period and horticulture increased from 16% to 26%. This reflects two shifts: one, out of subsidised field crops like maize into high-value food, vegetables and flowers, and the other into increasingly intensive forms of livestock production. These shifts mirror the changes in global agriculture.

The post-1994 land reform programme has not had much impact on the inherited agrarian structure. Around 3 million hectares have been redistributed to 186 000 people, while 2,6 million hectares have been restored through land restitution. About 1,5 million people have benefited from the programme, although the majority received only cash compensation. This means that only 5,6 million hectares (5% of agricultural land) has changed hands, and of the 1,7 million beneficiaries, probably only about 220 000 to 250 000 people actually received land. There are many reasons for this but it does point to the failure of the land reform programme.

Figure 9.3: Agrarian structure: Dualism and the 'missing middle'

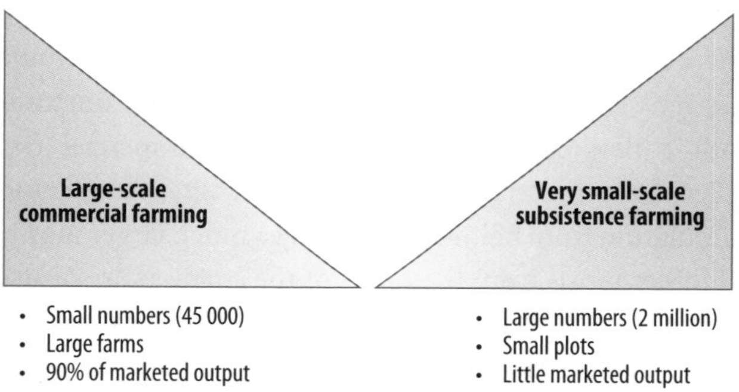

The lack of post-settlement support has been a major problem. At a land reform project I visited, women were trying to grow vegetables. They had never done this before and were given no advice. I watched as an agricultural expert from a local non-governmental organisation stood by while people tried to grow carrots by planting them in a seedbed and then transplanting them individually into rows, a completely counterproductive approach. This is prime agricultural land that cannot be put to good use without proper advice or training.

Figure 9.3 reflects a major problem in terms of this highly dualistic agrarian structure –the so-called 'missing middle'. At one end is large-scale commercial farming, where a relatively small number of large farms produce 90% of marketed output. The other extreme is small-scale subsistence farming, with large numbers of people, small plots and minimal marketed output.

The small-scale commercial farming sector does not get much attention in conventional thinking. There are about 200 000 smallholders who produce some marketed output on small farms. Do they constitute a 'missing middle' that could be increased in scale to reconfigure this sector and make a dent in rural poverty? Under the Mbeki administration, the idea was to promote emerging commercial farmers. Land reform policy was geared to support emerging farmers. Large-scale commercial farmers were supposed to provide a model and support, while also making the land available through the market. Recently, the debate has become framed in terms of different accumulation paths. Existing commercial farmers helping to nurture and mentor a new class of emerging black commercial farmers is called 'accumulation from above'. An alternative vision is 'accumulation from below': promoting a much larger number of smallholder farms from the ranks of the small-scale subsistence farmers to fill in this missing middle. Is it possible to have both?

Clearly, South Africa has a very dualistic system and extremely high levels of poverty. Employment in commercial agriculture has fallen over the years. The big question is whether, and how, farming can help to reduce rural poverty. Linked to that is the question of a potential role for agro-processing.

On the input side, the fertiliser sector was 'rationalised' in the 1990s, following deregulation and liberalisation. Four large corporations now dominate this sector: Sasol Nitro, Yara, Omnia and Foskor. South Africa has also become a net importer of fertilisers. About 70% of agro-chemicals are imported, which contributes to a cost-price squeeze for farmers. In the pesticide sector, eight of the ten largest multinationals operate in the South African market, which is dominated by Bayer, Dow and Syngenta. There are high levels of concentration in the supply of these basic inputs.

Farm finance was long seen as a developmental responsibility of the state, via the Land Bank and the agricultural credit facility. The Land Bank used to contribute large amounts but it ran into serious management problems and now contributes relatively little. Commercial banks have increasingly taken over the provision of agricultural finance.

The issue of seed production demonstrates the power of multinational companies. In the decade to 2007, wheat imports grew steadily from 20% to 60% of the total volume of consumption. Local production declined by 54% over the same period, from 1,38 million tonnes to 683 million tonnes, as it was displaced by imported wheat, mainly from Argentina. Part of the problem is that Monsanto, one of the largest agro-corporations in the world, purchased South Africa's wheat seed companies at the turn of the decade. Monsanto decided that it was not profitable to invest in improving seed varieties, complaining that farmers were saving seed. One consequence of this decision was the rapid decline in wheat production.

Concerning processing and packaging, the old cooperatives (with farmers as the major shareholders) were largely responsible for grain storage and milling. They handled the most important crops and supplied inputs to farmers. In 1995, the cooperatives had an asset value of R15 billion, with the top eight accounting for 45% of this amount. After the amendments to the Co-operatives Act in 1993, many were converted into private companies. Concentration increased over time: by 2002, three private silo companies, Senwes, Afgri and Noordwes owned 70% of all storage facilities. Afgri, the privatised Oos-Transvaal Koöperasie (OTK), claimed a 30% share of handling and storage capacity in 2009. The top four maize millers controlled 73% of the milling market in 2004.

The Competition Commission called for an analysis of mergers and acquisitions in the agro-processing sector from 1996 to 2006. The PLAAS study found significant activity by the former cooperatives. They acquired or merged with other companies to increase both horizontal integration (e.g. in the maize commodity chain, with large players extending into new regions) and vertical integration (e.g. in maize production, storage, milling, animal feed and poultry production). Afgri, in particular, is active in all of these sectors. Strategic diversification was another motive for mergers and acquisitions. For example, Pioneer, which was formed by the merger of two grain cooperatives, Sasko and Bokomo, became a diversified food manufacturing group.

Table 9.1: Concentration in the food processing sector, 1996

Major group and subgroup	No of firms	Relative contribution of		Herfindahl Hirschman index[1]
Meat, fish, fruit, vegetables, oils and fats	**480**	**0,1957**	**0,3678**	**188**
Slaughtering, dressing and packaging	149	0,4688	0,6358	661
Prepared and preserved meat	119	0,5591	0,7114	989
Canned, preserved and processed fish	46	0,5778	0,7924	1346
Canned and processed fruit and vegetables	157	0,3498	0,5497	482
Vegetables and animal oils and fats	16	0,6520	0,9779	1319
Dairy Products	**113**	**0,6843**	**0,8005**	**1598**
Processing of fresh milk	46	0,7079	0,8350	2430
Butter and cheese	17	0,8199	0,9743	1923
Ice cream and other edible ice	45	0,6007	0,7628	1293
Milk powder and other edible milk products	13	0,8700	0,9986	2742
Grain and mill products	**283**	**0,3604**	**0,5636**	**457**
Flour	209	0,4258	0,6481	648
Breakfast foods, starches and starch products	8	0,9544	–	3005
Prepared animal feeds	72	0,3727	0,6076	522
Other food products	**821**	**0,2613**	**0,5331**	**323**
Bakery products	522	0,4526	0,6262	609
Sugar, golden syrup and castor sugar	7	0,9856	–	3098
Cocoa, chocolates and sugar confectionary	72	0,7287	0,8237	1676

[1] Note: this is a commonly accepted measure of market concentration, calculated by summing the squared market share of each firm in the market. An index of between 1000 and 1800 represents a moderately concentrated market, while the score for a concentrated market is in excess of 1800.

Coffee, coffee substitutes and tea	15	0,8038	0,9580	2060
Nut foods	31	0,5129	0,7598	920
Other not elsewhere classified	182	0,3719	0,5012	471
Beverages	**163**	**0,4556**	**0,7455**	**760**
Distilling, rectifying and blending of spirits	97	0,6926	0,7812	1386
Beer and other malt liquors and malt	23	0,9195	0,9756	3777
Soft drinks; mineral waters	43	0,7355	0,9142	1876

Source: Vink & Kirsten (2002)

In general, the food processing sector is highly oligopolistic. Table 9.1 shows which particular products are moderately or highly concentrated. In 1976, 5% of firms controlled 65% of output; by 1996, it was 75%. In 1976, 10% of firms controlled 80% of output; this rose to 85% by 1996 (Fedderke & Szalontai, 2005). It has been argued that most of the concentration in food and beverage processing occurred before 1980. Vink and Kirsten (2002) suggest that, while the high levels of state support from the 1930s originally benefited farmers, large processing corporations benefited even more. Therefore, the concentration in the agro-food sector is nothing new.

Turning to wholesale and retail markets, the Chief Executive Officer of the Johannesburg Fresh Produce Market, Kgosientso Ramokgopa, said in an interview that the prices of fresh fruit and vegetables rose by an average of 84% between July 2008 and June 2009 (Barron, 2009). This increase was due to a huge retailer mark-up and was not passed on to farmers. For example, the wholesale price for 10 kg of potatoes was R32 but it retailed for R150. A second problem for farmers has been increasing input costs, partly because so many inputs are imported. Mr Ramokgopa also saw a growing trend of retailers buying direct from farmers. This has often meant that farmers are locked into fixed prices and onerous conditions of supply. Another concern has been the impact of the land claims process on production. Finally, the Johannesburg Fresh Produce Market has been sending out teams of inspectors to coach and advise emerging farmers – a job that the government should be doing.

Overall, Mr Ramokgopa spoke about pressure on wholesalers because of the market power of retailers. This points to the international 'supermarket revolution' (which South Africa itself is leading in Africa). The trends globally and locally include the following:

- Levels of market concentration are high, both horizontally and vertically (i.e. integrated procurement and supply).
- Companies use centralised procurement to ensure homogeneity of products, continuous delivery, stable shelf lives, and economies of scale via contracts and private standards.
- Specialised wholesalers are emerging, which are responsive to the needs of retailers.
- Companies use strategies, such as category management, that exert high levels of market power through procurement. For example, Shoprite organises its entire fresh produce supply through its Freshmark division.
- Certain suppliers may be preferred in order to simplify the movement of produce along the chain and to improve systems of quality control.
- High levels of concentration translate into low prices for farmers.
- Supermarkets are gradually penetrating the lower socio-economic segments of the market across the world.

These features can be found in most parts of the world, including China. This process is already advanced in South Africa and is spreading into Africa as Shoprite and others move into the region and even further afield. Shoprite, by the way, often sources its products in South Africa, which upsets farmers in places like Malawi.

The drivers for this global process include the following:

- Changing consumer demand (growing urban and middle class populations)
- Market liberalisation and deregulation
- Concentration of market power
- Competition among retailers
- Increasing quality and food safety standards
- New information technology for supply chain management
- Social and environmental responsibility.

Supermarkets controlled 66% of the South African retail food market in 2006. The four big players are Pick 'n Pay, Spar, Shoprite and Woolworths. There is much debate about the reason for rising food prices. Cutts and Kirsten (2006) show that the market power of retailers allows them, for certain products, to pass on only price increases to consumers but not decreases in price. This is the case for maize, wheat and long-life milk but not for sunflower oil (which is largely imported) or fresh milk, which is a perishable product. However, the main debate about food prices concerns the role of the large retailers, which is the subject of an investigation by the Competition Commission.

Figure 9.4 again shows the value chain from Figure 9.1 but indicates high levels of concentration with stars. On the input side, every category is highly concentrated. In South Africa, with only 45 000 large-scale commercial farmers in a rural population of maybe 16 million, farming itself may be seen as concentrated. However, there are particularly high levels of concentration in penned livestock (feedlots, poultry and pigs); high levels in processing and packaging, both primary and secondary; and very high levels in retail, especially the supermarkets.

Figure 9.4: Concentration in South Africa's agro-food regime

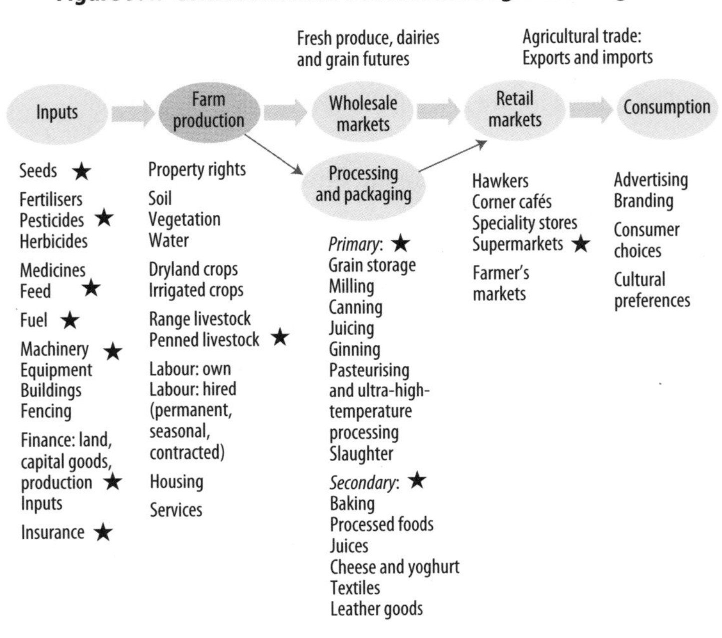

The entire agro-food regime in South Africa is dominated by small numbers of powerful players. Figure 9.5 portrays the concentration as an 'hourglass figure' with few input suppliers, larger numbers of farm producers, few processors and then large numbers of consumers.

Two more issues deserve attention: the global agro-food regime and the policy options. On the first issue, the book, *The global food economy: The battle for the future of farming*, by Canadian geographer Tony Weis (2007: 161–2) is fascinating. Everything he points to here can be seen globally on a more advanced scale, particularly in the industrial countries but increasingly across the world. His summary below resonates with the picture of South African agriculture:

> Since the 1970s, agro-TNCs [agricultural transnational corporations] have been the dominant forces transforming

Figure 9.5: The hourglass figure

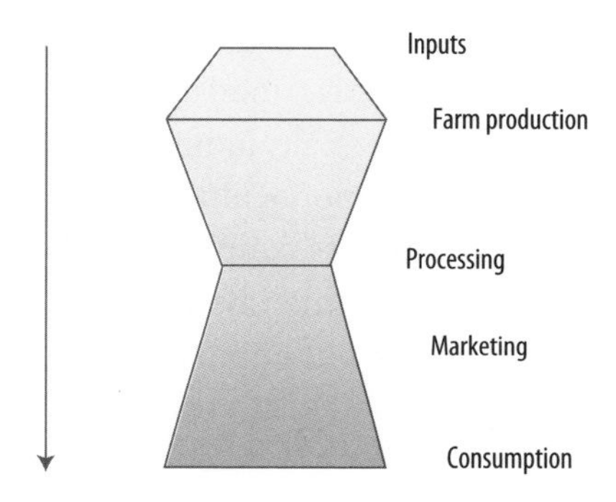

the nature of agriculture and integrating markets, horizontally across space and vertically through input and commodity chains. In their quest to increase markets and profits, agro-TNCs are relentlessly forging input dependence and standardising the nature of agricultural production, subjecting soaring farm animal populations to brutalising treatment, toxifying soils and water and externalising environmental costs, reshaping dietary aspirations, breaking local bonds between production and consumption, devalorising labour and replacing it with technology and progressively appropriating control and surplus value from farmers and farm communities.

Control and profits are instead centred in the complex and ever more despacialised corporate webs of agro-inputs, processing, distribution and retailing. This has trapped farmers in a rising (input) cost–falling (output) price squeeze, hurting the viability of small farms in both rich and poor countries… Amid this competitive squeeze, rising production has gone hand-in-hand with the polarisation of industrial farming, as small numbers of very large farmers have survived low margins by growing in scale and technology, with this growth assisted by both the uneven subsidy regimes in rich countries

> and by the indirect subsidisation that is implicit in the externalisation of its environmental costs.
>
> The booming productive model in the global food economy is thus the large-scale, industrialised, subsidised and fossil-fuel-intensive monoculture on a treadmill of agro-chemicals and fertilizers, coupled to (either directly or through an intermediary) intensive livestock production, typically of no more than one animal species. The flipside of this in consumption terms is the meatification of diets, or what Cockburn (1996: 27) describes as 'the surge in meat-eating associated with industrial capitalism'.

This analysis points to the dominance in world agriculture of what Harriet Friedmann calls the 'grain-livestock complex', where vast amounts of grain are produced primarily for animal feed, in particular maize and soya. Animals are produced intensively in feedlots, poultry batteries or pig houses, fed largely on grain – which is not their natural diet – and turned into fast food. Fast food outlets and supermarkets are promoting a particular lifestyle (and diet) that ultimately benefits the powerful players along the chain of industrialised agriculture.

A couple of important points emerge from this. First, the grain-livestock complex in, for example, the United States, Europe and Argentina is actually supported by sizeable state subsidies that benefit the large corporations more than the farmers; the farmers are increasingly under pressure. Second, food products for high-end consumers are particularly profitable; high-value food chains have grown as specific diet niches, such as fast foods, have become a 'lifestyle'. This lifestyle includes more consumption of meat, especially poultry. The 'meatification' of diets also has unfortunate health consequences. Just as it is not good for cattle to eat grain rather than grass, it is not good for humans to eat as much meat as they do. This raises significant questions about the long-term sustainability of this so-called 'productive industrial agriculture'. There has been a massive reaction against factory farming in certain parts of the world and among certain consumers, for three reasons: its extensive consumption of fossil fuels; its direct contribution to climate change; and its ecological consequences.

One of the results of this shift to integrated global agro-food markets is that any price shock ripples through the whole system. When food prices rose in early 2008, the impact was felt across the world. Currently, powerful countries and large corporations are looking to consolidate their sources of food. They find underutilised land in continents like Africa in order to secure their food supply through large-scale industrial production. This is the so-called 'land grab' phenomenon: the acquisition of large quantities of land by sovereign funds, companies and national governments for industrial farming. The perverse consequence is that South Africa is now 'exporting' commercial farmers to countries such as Libya, the Democratic Republic of Congo and Nigeria because they have skills in industrial large-scale agriculture. The farmers may even see this as a way of accessing the impressive amounts of state support they used to get from the apartheid government.

The changing nature of agriculture creates several knock-on effects that raise important questions for industrial policy in South Africa. The policy options outlined in the earlier presentation on value addition are entirely appropriate, but some additional options could be considered:

The first is land reform. Unlike in the industrial sector, the redistribution of assets in land and property rights is an available policy option in the agricultural sector. South Africa can promote 'accumulation from below' and poverty reduction for a certain number of smallholders or small-scale capitalist farmers. If there were 250 000 of them, rather than the current 45 000, there would be a major redistribution of income, with real benefits for maybe 1,5 million people.

The second policy option involves capping carbon emissions and implementing the cap-and-trade method. For sustainable systems to be put in place, environmental costs have to be externalised. In a democratic society, there may be only one way to achieve this: obtain scientific agreement on the allowable levels of emission and then tax, cap or control them.

The third option is to create alternative systems of production using green technologies. Organic crops should also be a policy option, although this type of farming needs high levels of skill and large amounts of biomass.

South Africa needs to reintegrate crops and livestock and reconfigure its farming systems. This is not a reversion to less sophisticated forms of agriculture. Instead, it is more sophisticated, finding ways to build on natural cycles or loops of nutrients and water rather than using the 'industrial throughput' style. This is a demanding task, which has significant consequences for agro-processing and other pro-employment industrial policies.

Much remains to be done but once agriculture has been reconfigured, change will occur along the whole chain. South Africa needs to think about relationships between players and, more importantly, about the way that systems of consumption are ultimately related to ways of producing. Everything is interlinked from input supply to production and consumption. Changes in one part of the chain require other parts to change as well. That is both exciting and challenging.

References

Barron, C, 2009. Bumper harvest thanks to hard work, *The Times*, 21 November. www.timeslive.co.za/business/article203002.ece/Bumper-harvest-thanks-to-hard-work

Cutts, M & Kirsten, J, 2006. Asymmetric price transmission and market concentration: An investigation into four South African agro-food industries, *South African Journal of Economics*, 74:2.

Fedderke, J & Szalontai, G, 2005. *Industry concentration in South African manufacturing industry: Trends and consequences, 1972–96.* Economic Research Southern Africa Working Paper 23. Cape Town: University of Cape Town.

Vink, N & Kirsten, J, 2002. *Pricing behaviour in the South African food and agricultural sector*. Report to the Treasury. www.sarpn.org.za/documents/d0000327/P280_Pricing.pdf

Vorley, B, Fearne, A & Ray, D (eds), 2007. *Re-governing markets: A place for small-scale producers in modern agrifood chains?* Abingdon, UK: Gower Publishing. www.regoverningmarkets.org

Weis, T, 2007. *The global food economy: The battle for the future of farming.* London: Zed Books.

Part Three

Potential Resources for Development

Opening remarks

Ben Turok

In the first seminar, Neva Makgetla made a presentation on 'The structure of the economy'. Everybody says that the structure of the economy has not changed. But what is the structure? It relates to the core economic institutions and includes features like ownership, production, spatial factors and the allocation of resources to education and skills. These issues are now of concern because of the persistence of high levels of joblessness and inequality in the South African economy. Clearly, amelioration in modest increments will not work if the structure is not addressed.

It is interesting to see that the Green Paper on Planning agrees that the economic structure has not changed for a hundred years, but then there is no follow-up. Planning is based not on restructuring but on other considerations. Similarly, many documents acknowledge that the structure has not changed but do not say what needs to change.

Neva talked about the question of capital inflows as opposed to domestic capital, and stressed the centrality of the question of class. Class is the missing dimension of many discussions on economics; government documents certainly do not talk about it. Therefore, this series includes the class dimension, which forms part of the inherited structural legacy.

The next topic was the concentration in the manufacturing, finance, retail and telecommunications industries, and the need to track the development of capital. If I may insert a bit of my own thinking on this, despite making enquiries for months, I did not find a single reference to an article that delineates the architecture of capital in South Africa. Even McGregor's *Who owns whom* does not show the architecture of the whole industry. It is important to track the development of capital in South Africa in order to understand the existing architecture. Linked to this are issues such as the massive expansion of private capital, the privatisation of services and their market dominance, the state-owned enterprises, and state capital in the development finance institutions and the PIC.

Looking forward, what will be *the main driver* of the economy? What is the main driver now and what is it likely to be in the future? Since the 1969 Morogoro conference, the ANC position has always been that poverty will not change without a change in the structure of the economy. Political changes are certainly not enough; the structure must change. It is strange that, in 16 years, neither the government nor the ANC has seriously discussed the question of restructuring the inherited structure.

The second seminar looked at the main areas of mining, manufacturing, agriculture, services and finance, around issues of ownership and control, and production and distribution. One of the principal points was the financialisation of the South African economy, which has contributed to concentration, undermined investment in the industrial sector, and fuelled a debt-driven consumer boom. The conclusion seems to be that value added is rather low in South Africa. This is the reason why jobs are not being created, which explains the high levels of unemployment and poverty. On the other hand, pervasive rent seeking also contributes to inequality and the poor performance of the economy. The levels of rent seeking and added value really need to be addressed for the economy to make progress.

A final question that emerges is, 'Can we move towards a strong developmental state?' That seems to be the governing idea for the whole exercise.

10. Potential resources for development

Rob Davies

This presentation highlights two important themes from the newly released Industrial Policy Action Plan (IPAP 2 of 2010) to speak to the theme of 'potential resources for development'.

South Africa needs to make structural changes to the real economy in order to address the pressing problems of inequality, poverty and unemployment. The focus of the IPAP is the value-adding sectors. These include manufacturing and some services sectors, particularly those with a link to manufacturing. These sectors will not necessarily create all the jobs that need to be created but there is no case in economic history where rising incomes, growing employment and declining inequality were *not* driven by the value-adding sectors. This is the challenge that the country must face.

South Africa's growth path has been driven by unsustainable consumption. The sectors that provide services or goods for credit purchases have grown much faster than the productive sectors – at an average annual rate of 7,7%, as against 2,9% for the productive sectors. South Africa is importing goods for consumption rather than producing them, which contributes to the widening deficit on the current account.

Manufacturing accounts for about 54% of the production side of the economy and its performance there is quite critical. Another consequence of the current growth path has been the inability to address the problem of structural unemployment.

South Africa lost 900 000 jobs in the recession; this was a cyclical problem. But, even at the height of the growth between 2005 and 2007, unemployment never fell below 22.8% of the economically active population. Without resuscitating the production side and placing it on a growth path characterised by increasing returns, South Africa will not be able to create the decent jobs that are needed.

The lacklustre performance of the manufacturing sector is due to various constraints, which have to be addressed in a comprehensive way. The first one is currency volatility and, at least recently, a significant overvaluation of the currency relative to comparator countries. The uncompetitive exchange rate has damaged the productive sector.

South Africa also has a high cost of capital relative to its competitors – in particular in the industrial sector – with private credit not being extended to the production sectors. Public capital and other infrastructure investments have not been adequately leveraged for their industrial development opportunities. Vital intermediate inputs in the industrial sector are priced opportunistically. Two well-known problems need attention: infrastructure and the skills system.

These are the overall diagnoses in the IPAP. None of these is necessarily new but the IPAP suggests some new treatments, both crosscutting and sectoral measures. It argues as follows:

A comprehensive and integrated policy response is required to scale up industrial policy:

- Stronger coherence between macro- and microeconomic policies in relation to exchange and interest rates, inflation and trade balance imperatives
- Industrial financing channelled to more labour-intensive and value-adding sectors
- Leveraging procurement to raise domestic production and employment in a range of sectors
- Developmental trade policies, such as tariffs and standards deployed in a selective and strategic manner

- Competition policies: competitive input costs for productive investments and affordable goods and services for poor and working-class households
- Skills, technology and innovation policies better aligned to sectoral priorities
- Deploying these policies in general and in relation to more ambitious sector strategies, as set out in detailed crosscutting and sector key action plans.

Two of these deserve mention. The first is the challenge of allocating more affordable capital for investment in industrial development through, in particular, the development finance institutions. The other area is proposals for leveraging public procurement.

The current profile of finance in the economy shows huge growth in the finance sector and involvement in various financial services. There has been a significant expansion of mortgage advances, leasing, store finance and other loan advances, while financing for investment is the small part at the bottom of the graph. The trend was downward even before the onset of the recession. Private investment has been going first to general government services and the infrastructure programme, then to certain service sectors, and then to basic chemicals, non-metallic minerals and so on. Even those investments, determined by profitability, have been concentrated in the more capital-intensive sectors in the minerals-energy complex.

The cost and availability of capital have long been critical constraints for investment, especially in the industrial sector. South Africa's cost of capital is among the highest of its partners and comparative countries, and the terms are not competitive. Recent improvements in investment rates have been driven by public investment.

Comparable countries and emerging economies that are more successful have at least one thing in common – development banks that play a critical role in channelling development finance to productive activities. South Korea's Development Bank or Brazil's BNDES are good examples. Over the last few years, the dti and the IDC have interacted with Brazil to learn lessons from its experience. A stream of work is being undertaken to create ongoing concessional funding on a larger scale; this is a key action plan in the IPAP.

Table 10.1 on the following page compares two development banks: the IDC and BNDES. The IDC provides concessional funding for industrial development but its balance sheet has not been topped up with public funds since the 1950s. It leverages its mature assets in existing – usually capital-intensive – industries and combines this with funds raised on a commercial basis.

BNDES, on the other hand, has a regular inflow of additional funding from the Workers' Assistance Fund (FAT). This job creation fund differs from South Africa's Unemployment Insurance Fund in that does not directly support the unemployed – there is another fund for that. About 40% of it goes to BNDES, which pays back only the interest and not the capital. BNDES also floats treasury bonds on attractive terms. This regular inflow of funding enlarges the capital base and enables BNDES to offer loans on terms that are better than those of the IDC, even though interest rates in Brazil are higher than in South Africa.

Within two quarters of the IPAP coming into force, two things need to happen. The first is a serious discussion with the IDC about further leveraging its existing balance sheet and the second is to conceptualise a sustainable regular flow of funding into the IDC along the lines of – but not identical to – BNDES.

The second concerns the leveraging of procurement. South Africa is involved in a major and growing programme of infrastructure investment, despite the perception that it was only for the Soccer World Cup and would decrease afterwards. In fact, infrastructure investment will increase rather than decrease. However, South Africa has not been generating industrial opportunities from this programme. There has been growing

Table 10.1: Comparison of the IDC and BNDES

Indicators	IDC, South Africa	BNDES, Brazil
Source of loan financing	• Commercial bank loans • Loans from commercial development finance institutions	• Workers' Assistance Fund (FAT) – Legislatively mandated flow of large portion of FAT (+40%) – BNDES repays only interest, not capital • Treasury bonds on attractive terms
Structure of loan financing		
Long-term interest rate	8,8%	6,25% (TJLP)
Basic spread	1%	0% to 3% (average approx. 1,09%)
Credit risk levy	0% to 4%	0,46% to 3,57%
Average credit risk levy (approximate)	1,7%	1%
Real interest rate of loans		
Average lending rate	11,5%	8,34%
Real bank rate	4,92%	7,61%
Real interest rate	6,58%	0,73%

investment by the government and the public corporations in infrastructure, but the balance of trade is deteriorating sharply, which presents a serious challenge. These industries should be supplying the inputs for the infrastructure programmes, instead of importing them. The new IPAP has been developed to address these concerns.

The current arrangements for public procurement do not support local manufacturing. The Department of Public Enterprises collects data on procurement by state-owned enterprises. It is clear from the data that South African industries should have been able to supply much of the requirements without any support. Instead, most of those components had to be imported.

Currently, public procurement is not conducted strategically; each procurement process is treated separately as a discrete exercise. Suppose a municipality wants to invest in a bus rapid transit system; it only puts Phase 1 out for tender. The contractor for Phase 1 will probably want to import the buses because of limited local capacity. When the municipality gets to Phase 2, it puts out a separate tender and probably comes to the same conclusion. This way, the possibilities of the overall process are not harnessed and no strategic medium- and long-term procurement plans are created. In Brazil, by contrast, the phases are linked. Although the contractor who wins Phase 1 may have to import, by Phase 2, the same contractor is expected to achieve a certain proportion of local procurement. This proportion is again increased in Phase 3. This is an example of medium- to long-term 'fleet procurement'. Fleet procurement involves bigger and longer-term procurements that combine the different phases of a project into a single contract.

Public procurement currently gives little or no price advantage to local production. The IPAP proposes a number of measures to strengthen this, although the first examples will be modest. Working with the state-owned enterprises and the Department of Public Enterprises, the dti will identify about eight or ten products for fleet procurement. The text box gives examples of these.

Identification of strategic procurement 'fleets' for the explicit development of long-term procurement plans that incorporate requirements for local production and supplier development:

- Locomotives, wagons or coaches for freight and commuter rail
- Key elements of the coal-fired electricity build programme
- Key elements of the nuclear electricity build programme
- Buses procured by metropolitan municipalities
- Components or materials in relation to aerospace procurement by South African Airways and the South African National Defence Force

- Appropriate sequencing of inclusion of pharmaceuticals, especially anti-retrovirals
- Set-top boxes for the digital migration process

Source: Minister's briefing (2010: Slide 27)

Most of these examples are illustrative but rail locomotives are close to being placed into fleet procurement. Buses for metropolitan municipalities will require some changes in legislation. The state will address the question whether the NIPP applies to local government. Also, procurement legislation and practice will be overhauled and discretionary points in the BEE codes aligned with local procurement.

The government wants to eliminate 'import fronting', which usually means that a black person who is not actually the manager of a company is presented as such for the company to qualify for BEE projects. This is a clear form of fraud but there are at least two other types of fronting. One is 'tenderpreneuring', where a (real) black-owned company does not do the work stipulated in the contract but subcontracts it instead to another (probably white-owned) company and charges the government a premium for that. The other form is 'import fronting'. Here, the black company, in the name of BEE, imports goods rather than use a white-owned South African company that produces the goods locally. In a recent case, a municipality procured cables overseas through a BEE procurement; this led to a thousand jobs being lost at a local cable company. These forms of fronting will also be combated.

Another proposal for leveraging procurement is to allow price matching for domestic producers: when an importer quotes a particular price, the domestic producer will be given an opportunity to match it.

Two pieces of legislation or regulation currently cover procurement. The first, the Competitive Supplier Development Programme (CSDP), requires Transnet and Eskom procurers to work with local manufacturers; in the longer term, this will be in their interest. This programme has made some progress but more needs to be done. The second is the NIPP, which relates to all procurements of US$10 million or more and requires some form of offset arrangement. It is not clear whether the NIPP covers all spheres of government; this needs to be addressed. Also, agencies have often awarded the contract first and then tried to negotiate the offset afterwards, by which time they had no leverage. Another concern is that the offset investment does not need to be in the contractor's sector – it could be in any sector. The South African government would prefer offsets to be in the same sector as the contractor.

The dti wants to start with fleet procurement. Next, in the medium term, regulatory reform will align BEE with the industrial development policy and seek to strengthen the capacity of development finance institutions to lock in domestic and regional procurement. The 'Proudly South African' campaign will also need to be revamped. There are two elements here. The first is to recognise local production. The 'Proudly South African' campaign should work with the South African National Accreditation System (SANAS), which is an accreditation services centre, to equip local producers to participate in state procurement. This would also make it more worthwhile for companies to become members of the campaign. Also, 'Proudly South African' would have to raise the profile of its campaigns to influence not only consumers but also procurement.

While this is the general purpose of the programme, these elements will become customised and integral to the industrial policy plan of each sector of focus. For example, procurement is fundamental to the growth of the metals fabrication, capital equipment and transport equipment sectors. Harnessing the benefits of procurement will allow those sectors to grow. This will create a new industrial development thrust to position South Africa to supply projects on the African continent (and even further afield) in the longer term.

The government also focuses on green industries, such as solar water heating, concentrated solar power, wind power and energy efficiency. Once these regulations are in place, together with tighter procurement policies, South Africa will be able to 'green' the economy and reap more opportunities for industrial development. The country aims for the 'greener' end of production value chains across the board in its industries.

Discussion

The participants accepted that the IPAP2 is a good start towards a 'suitable' industrial policy. As a first step, it aligns both public procurement and concessionary development finance with the overall goals of industrial policy. More challenging issues remain for later, such as the strategic use of standards and tariffs. While noting that industrial policy should not be overloaded, as it is not the totality of the growth path, the participants addressed the need to increase employment and the IPAP 2's apparent dichotomy between the consumption and productive sectors.

The participants argued, first, that a dichotomy between 'consumption and non-consumption' is not helpful. The economy should not be divided into 'productive' and 'non-productive' parts without understanding that the 'non-productive' sectors are needed to create jobs, even as the 'productive' core is needed for faster growth. There was an extraordinarily high rate of elasticity in employment creation relative to GDP during the boom. Much of that was due to the huge multiplier effect on the services sector. Sectors such as health, education and tourism create jobs, are major exporters and are good for the balance of payments, even though they are not creating material goods. Primarily because of jobs created in these sectors, unemployment fell by 25% in five years. (This was a significant decline but the economy had started at extremely high levels of unemployment by international standards.)

In response, it was argued that IPAP 2 does not exclude the services sector – it includes some services and does not make a categorical distinction between manufacturing and services. It does argue that the employment growth in services is unsustainable without a better performance from manufacturing. Jobs in the manufacturing sector are only a modest part of the total but every case of successful economic growth with decent work has come through an improved performance by the value-adding sectors.

The dti is aware that many jobs will come from the service sectors. However, without an expanding productive base, procurement for investment will translate into high imports, which will affect the balance of payments. In such a scenario, service jobs will be fragile and probably not sustainable. A dynamic value-added sector will drive a different dynamic in the services sectors, and even the primary sectors, and create more opportunities for decent work. Erik Reinert's book, *How rich countries got rich… and why poor countries stay poor* (2008) delves deep into economic history, back to the principality of Venice, and finds that none of the rich economies got there without an industrial policy. He also raises another interesting question: why are hotel workers in Peru paid much less than hotel workers in Norway? It is not because they do anything intrinsically different but because the average level of wages in Norway is much higher and it brings everybody along, even hotel workers.

A second set of issues, which forms part of the broader discourse, relates to the inherited (and systematically reproducing) inequalities in the economy and the need to identify and support labour-absorbing sectors. The sector analysis in the IPAP 2 needs to look more at the causes of low employment. It is agreed that the spectrum of manufacturing is part of the problem (i.e. the large role of refining and smelting), while the structure of the individual sectors also limits labour absorption. In each of the sectors, the government is trying to tilt towards more labour-absorbing paths, greener paths, and so on. In the automotive industry, for example, the Automotive Production and Development Programme (former MIDP) provides investment support for the original equipment manufacturers. Bus and capital equipment manufacturers have been invited into the programme as well. Several options that are not shown in detail in the IPAP 2 (e.g. collective procurement of some components) will boost the component manufacturing industry. Investments must be guided into the green economy and green motor vehicles. The carbon tax will make green cars more attractive.

The IPAP 2 supports some highly capital-intensive sectors. What about sectors that are *less* capital-intensive, especially those that appear to be 'unproductive', like most of the services sectors? What about upgrading informal workers? The solutions of the IPAP 2 are constructive but more needs to be done to support employment creation and equity to avoid the danger of creating a high-tech manufacturing sector. The growth path needs to look at employment and identify which sectors can actually create jobs.

The 'first and second economy' idea used in the past included the notion of 'ladders' to encourage people to move from the second economy to the first economy but only a very small minority of people could ever have done that. The sort of shift that is now envisaged, which will probably come out in the growth path document, is to improve the income-generating quality of productive activities. Even though these activities will stay in the informal sector for now, this will be a significant boost to growth. Some parts of the 'social economy' – the non-profit sector, cooperatives and the like – are actually critical. Although this does not form part of IPAP 2, it will be on the agenda of the dti.

Third, concerning concessionary finance, there has not been a significant shift in the allocation of the IDC's resources. Even though it has diversified into tourism and other labour-intensive services, the bulk of its support is for traditional capital-intensive industry. The question of the allocation of the IDC's resources is the first phase of a process. Further questions to consider are the status of its balance sheet, its leveraging powers and the support it offers. Defining the IPAP 2 sectors at least gives some signal of what answers will be required. The pressure will be to ensure greater employment in the sectors and subsectors that the IDC supports.

The MIDP cannot be replicated across the board nor can it be withdrawn without the loss of significant industrial capacity. Concessional funding through development finance institutions will probably be the main form of support to the other sectors. Industrial policy objectives will increasingly be reflected in the conditionalities and reciprocities of every form of support, whether on- or off-budget. These include additional investment, local procurement and employment creation.

Finally, the alignment of macro- and microeconomic policies is clearly a critical issue that the IPAP addresses. The Harvard Group recommended a competitive value for the currency; the mandate of the Reserve Bank has now been broadened to include that.

References

Economic Sectors and Employment Cluster (South Africa). 2010a. *2010/11–2012/13 Industrial Policy Action Plan* [IPAP]. www.dti.gov.za/ipap/IPAP2010-2013_18_FEB_2010.pdf

Economic Sectors and Employment Cluster (South Africa). 2010b. Minister's briefing to the Parliamentary Portfolio Committee, *2010/11–2012/13 Industrial Policy Action Plan*. www.thedti.gov.za/parlimentary/022310_Min_briefing_revised_ipap.pdf

Reinert, E, 2008. *How rich countries got rich… and why poor countries stay poor*. London: Constable.

11. Institutional issues

Ravi Naidoo

The term 'institution' will be used in this presentation to refer to structures and mechanisms of the State that affect implementation. To provide further analytical depth to this brief input, more attention will be paid to the institutional issues as they apply to one implementing agent, the DBSA.

The DBSA has three main functions. It is a development finance institution (DFI) with a statutory mandate to finance infrastructure in southern Africa. It is 100% owned by government with a Governor, the Minister of Finance as representative of its shareholder. From an initial R200 million injection from the government in 1983 the DBSA has grown its assets to R45,1 billion today. Unlike a government department and in common with most DFIs, the DBSA raises its own funds using its balance sheet, including issuing bonds to domestic and international investors. Despite the global recession, DBSA disbursed R8,3 billion in 2009/10 with R18,8 billion of financing approved for the year (roughly one third of financing is to the rest of the southern Africa region). In addition, in that same year, DBSA deployed 189 engineers and technicians, 80 finance experts, 26 planners, 156 young professionals and 164 artisans into hundreds of municipalities and government departments to support the implementation of infrastructure projects and address the skills constraint faced by local government institutions. Having the State as its main client since the 1980s, a comparative advantage of the DBSA's is this extensive knowledge of State implementation, enabling it to play an advisory role to government. That experience of state implementation informs this input.

On the institutional side, the DBSA has been considering the developmental state and its most important prerequisites. While the DBSA has traditionally been focused on financing socio-economic infrastructure programmes of the State, it has increasingly sought to examine and improve the planning systems that inform, and ultimately, determine these strategic choices. These choices, their sequence of implementation, and how they are executed have fundamental implications for the success or failure of the South African State.

Based on DBSA analysis, there are three core elements to a successful Developmental State.

The first is a planning system and centre to resolve contestation over decision-making. There is now, finally, an acceptance that at the macro level, South Africa needs an improved planning system and centre. Importantly, in addition to the technocratic function of assembling a long-term development path there has to be a Cabinet function that will resolve the contestation over decision-making in government. The National Planning Commission was intended to resolve some of those tensions, though it appears that its focus would be primarily on long-term plans only. However, in respect to short- and medium-term plans the performance contracting process led by the also newly created Ministry for Performance Monitoring and Evaluation could be a decisive factor. That said, unresolved contestation over decision-making remains a prevalent and persistent challenge.

The second requirement is to identify a 'critical path' for long-term development. DBSA has often developed 'roadmaps' for sectoral interventions (such as with health and basic education) that then guides the development of a government programme

Figure 11.1: Elements of a successful Developmental State

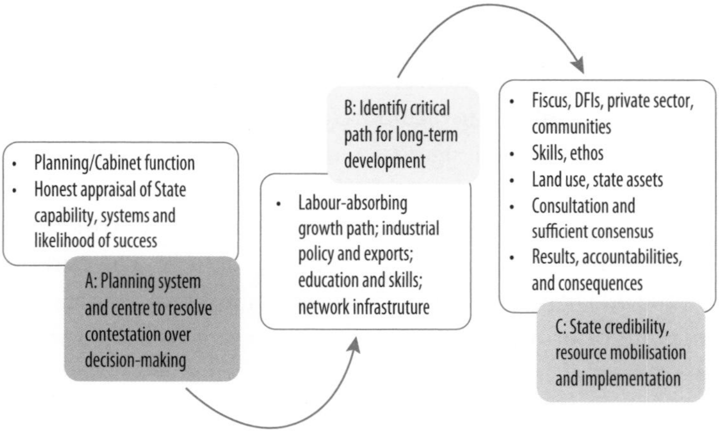

- Planning/Cabinet function
- Honest appraisal of State capability, systems and likelihood of success

A: Planning system and centre to resolve contestation over decision-making

B: Identify critical path for long-term development

- Labour-absorbing growth path; industrial policy and exports; education and skills; network infrastruture

- Fiscus, DFIs, private sector, communities
- Skills, ethos
- Land use, state assets
- Consultation and sufficient consensus
- Results, accountabilities, and consequences

C: State credibility, resource mobilisation and implementation

Source: DBSA own analysis, 2010

of action. At a national- or macro-level a roadmap is needed for South Africa's overall development agenda. Clearly such a roadmap must substantively include a labour-absorbing growth path, industrial and export policies, education and skills, and network infrastructure.

In specific bureaucratic parlance, it will engage and incorporate various initiatives of government such as the National Planning Commission work, the New Growth Path, the Industrial Policy Action Plan 2, the anti-poverty strategy and so forth. There are obviously tensions, contradictions and trade-offs between and amongst this mix of initiatives that have to be resolved. Taking the path of least resistance, such as simply putting all proposals on the same to-do list, would be the most convenient and ultimately the worst approach. There may be things that government wants to do, or is inspired to do, but that it is not ready to do. If a structural transformation of the current growth path is to be achieved, tough choices, some unpopular at this time, will have to be made.

Currently, the resolution to this macro-roadmap process is unclear. However institutions such as the DBSA – with its infrastructure focus – which must make decisions that will endure for decades thereafter – do not have the luxury of operating in a planning vacuum. Decisions made today have to be justifiable in view of longer-term developmental considerations.

In 2009, the first year of the then-new administration, DBSA produced *Towards a Long-Term Development Path* (LTDP). It was a new initiative of the DBSA but an essential one. The purpose of the LTDP was to identify interventions that government *ought* to prioritise in the three five-year terms to 2025 if it was to successfully achieve the goals it had stated at the time. Apart from being of use in its engagement with government, it would also serve DBSA as an in-house guide to development priorities and their sequencing. The essence of the LTDP is reflected in Figure 11.2.

The LTDP analysis above is not an attempt at a blueprint for the future. Indeed, predicting the future is a perilous and dangerous exercise that is generally to be avoided. Predictions and cast-in-stone blueprints however should not be confused with having a development vision and knowing how you will achieve that vision in practice. Having a vision and a rough set of implementation plans subject to change as conditions change (i.e. a 'long-term development path') is actually an essential task for the State. That South Africa has muddled through since 1994 without a long-term development path is itself a remarkable if unpleasant fact, and goes some way to explaining some of the more structural challenges that the country has now started to run into.

The third element of a successful Developmental State is that none of the planning will amount to much if the state is not credible. Given the dispersed characteristics of power and resources in South Africa it is unlikely that implementation can be centrally determined. Resource mobilisation and

Figure 11.2: Establishing a set of long-term goals and doable targets

A possible sequencing of development path priorities to 2025		
2009–2014	**2015–2019**	**2020–2025**
1. Prioritise the implementation of growth-enhancing public works programmes, especially with a view to create employment opportunities (e.g. maintaining network infrastructure). 2. Improve the performance of the public service to play a central role in development, focusing most on management and system changes in key services and districts. 3. Increase the potential of the private and non-State sectors to generate growth and employment through promoting economic efficiencies. 4. Improve policy coordination and coherence within government as a basis for improved performance and policy certainty within key investor communities.	1. Priotise the promotion of high employment linkage sectors, geared largely to domestic and regional markets. 2. Strengthen 'reception' strategies to support the gradual in-migration to urban areas. 3. Strengthen rural development programmes through quality basic service delivery and specific sector strategies. Systemic solutions for unsustainable rural municipalities. 4. Embed public service mandarin and merit-system through the development of a core layer of senior management.	1. Based on improved basic education, substantially bigger investments in higher education. 2. With gradual increase in employment, shift more attention to scaling up high-tech industries. 3. Continue to improve performance in public service, through adopting ISO-standards. 4. Continued focus on economic efficiencies with improvements against international benchmarks. 5. Climate change interventions become more ambitious, such as carbon tax implementation.

Source: DBSA, 2009

implementation depend heavily on the credibility of the State – defining how to mobilise the fiscus, State assets such as land, social and cultural resources, development finance institutions, the private sector, communities and other partners. If there is a high degree of confidence and trust, key role players are more likely to commit resources in practice. Where the credibility of the main initiator is low, slow adoption and excuses for non-participation will be prevalent.

Leadership is obviously important, in terms of mobilising not just the state but also building a social compact. A core function of leadership will be to ensure that the State actually delivers on its promises, beginning with its side of any social compact. As key stakeholders see the State go beyond statements of intent to action (and consequences for delivery or the lack thereof), there is a high probability that the credibility and resource mobilisation of the State will increase accordingly. In a sense, success begets success – and the aspirant Developmental State can then achieve a critical mass enabling it to live up to that aspirant title.

Taking the earlier discussion forward, we can now delve deeper into mobilising resources and implementation for infrastructure development. Figure 11.3 sets out some of the key considerations.

It is generally accepted that infrastructure programmes must be at the core of government plans. Infrastructure programmes sustained economic growth in the recent economic crisis and, with R872 billion of spending over the medium-term expenditure period (until 2013/14), will be a key driver of growth in the future. The network infrastructure that is established will be a basis for future growth of the economy and ensure that the State meets its Constitutional requirement to progressively realise socio-economic rights.

How will the State fund its infrastructure requirements? Either it pays for it directly from the central government fiscus or the various infrastructure entities (e.g. the transport parastatal, Transnet) raise their funds through borrowing from the market. Clearly the more income-generating and enabling the infrastructure programmes are, the more likely it is that the longer-term revenue base of the country will be increased to enable the debt to be repaid.

Important in this equation is the source of funds for such infrastructure programmes. From whom will the State borrow

Figure 11.3: System-wide perspective of resource mobilisation for infrastructure

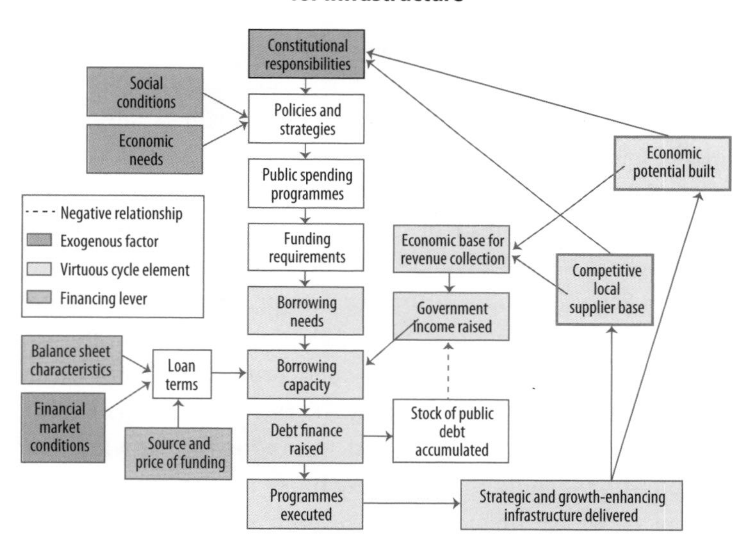

Source: DBSA own analysis, 2010

for this infrastructure? Lessons derived from the experience of successful Developmental States in East Asia are instructive. There, the domestic savings-priority investment nexus was critical. Domestic savings, such as through provident and pension funds, were blended with donor funds to offer the lowest price debt possible to finance key infrastructure programmes. The extent to which the South African pension and provident fund industry, including the considerable government employees' pensions, can be mobilised to support infrastructure programmes is therefore an important consideration for South Africa.

There are ways to ensure that savings are protected whilst support is being provided to strategic programmes. Indeed South Africa has R780 billion just in the Government Employees Pension Fund alone. The Fund is invested in financial markets and can make a good return, though when markets tumble it stands to lose much of its value. However the Fund is already full-funded (meaning it has enough capital to pay off all its current and future liabilities) and the State already guarantees the pensions due to retiring members. Hence, it can be argued that the Fund needs security and smooth earnings rather than higher and volatile growth.

Is there a way to make these funds part of the development finance system? Instead of chasing higher returns which the Fund does not need, it could rather be deployed in full or part to support State-guaranteed infrastructure programmes. The funds could thus contribute to actual development and have smooth, secure long-term returns. In this model the more senior of the State development finance intermediaries with excellent credit ratings – such as the DBSA and the Industrial Development Corporation – could manage these funds on tight performance contracts whilst financing the respective infrastructure and industrial priorities.

The mobilisation of resources for infrastructure goes beyond what infrastructure the State targets and how it goes about sourcing finance for it. It is also about how these infrastructure projects are undertaken. Infrastructure projects that make more use of local-labour and encourage the development of competitive local suppliers is clearly preferable. Every infrastructure programme uses literally thousands of suppliers, and each of these is a potential industry. Gradually creating space for competitive local suppliers to break into these markets could, over a reasonable period, see some of these competitive local suppliers become significant exporters and job-creators in the future and establish new productive sectors in the economy.

Government and state-owned enterprises that undertake the actual infrastructure programmes need to review their procurement systems in this regard, to consider appropriate incentives and support programmes for local suppliers. In some cases, our rules inadvertently may have made it easier or cheaper to import goods and services (often subsidised by foreign countries), so the entire set of incentives for procurement needs to be reviewed to facilitate support for local suppliers while ensuring that costs do not become too excessive.

Over the full-life cycle of the infrastructure assets there are also massive opportunities for maintenance and construction work. As South Africa spends only 20% of the amount required for maintenance, assets are prone to deteriorating faster than they should. This is extremely wasteful and a sign of planning that is neither long-term nor integrated. The net result is that South Africa must then use scarce resources on new infrastructure that would not have been required had the existing infrastructure been properly maintained. The failure of maintenance programmes of the past, however, represents a maintenance opportunity for the future. Maintenance work, while saving the State billions in infrastructure costs, is often a labour-intensive programme that can even draw in local communities (such as for maintaining rural, off-grid infrastructure).

Let us now go deeper into the operating environment of one set of implementing actors, the DFIs. There is no doubt that state-owned enterprises and development finance institutions have made significant commitments to many infrastructure programmes. However, the ability to raise funding overseas plummeted in the midst of the global recession, imposing real constraints to financing programmes.

Consider the DBSA. Its governing Act prescribes a debt-to-equity limit of 250%. Because it is taking on more of the State infrastructure programme, the Bank will breach that limit in the next two years, reaching over 300%. To some degree, the same holds for some of the other development finance institutions. This motivated the Minister of Finance in 2009 to extend a further R15,2 billion guarantee to the DBSA, taking its total State guarantee to R20 billion. Though not actual cash, if treated as equity it now enables the DBSA to raise more debt without contravening its legislated requirements.

This then raises the issue of the balance sheets of the development finance institutions, which show wide variations. South Africa has 14 national development finance institutions and more than a dozen major provincial ones. These institutions need to work together to coordinate financing and investments, ensure a high development impact and contribute to the countercyclical strategy around development. Indeed, how many of them are really making the impact that the country needs them to?

And how should the provincial development finance institutions relate to the national ones? Perhaps because provincial institutions have more knowledge of their local areas, they could focus on local firms whilst the national DFIs are mandated to run the national programmes. Provincial DFIs, for example, could provide bridging finance to provincial firms so they can take up projects (on tender) supporting the provincial development programmes.

However it is done, the coordination and management of the development finance institutions as a group is vital. All DFIs need to balance their different tasks: they have to be financially sustainable, have a development impact, and be well governed. In addition each DFI should have its own distinctive competencies. It is important that they are given direction and, at the same time, be allowed to find their own sustainability. At present, there is an opportunity for better management of the system.

Let us now look at the public service, a much more important implementing actor than a DFI. When we discuss the need for 'better management' of resources within the State, the question of efficiency and effectiveness of the public service is of course paramount. As a resource, the performance trajectory of the sheer mass of the public service human and financial resources will make or break development in South Africa. With employees exceeding one million and overseeing a budget of one trillion Rand, a focused and effective public service can be a major tool for development. Conversely a low-productivity public service can have a draining and deadening effect on the growth and development potential of the country. Indeed, giving more powers and functions to such a body, without first ensuring its performance is being improved, would be to make many a bad situation worse. Rather than overly sophisticated strategies and initiatives, it could be argued that a priority is to attain a 'working State' – a generalised level of adequate performance. (Naidoo, 2009)

Beyond public infrastructure programmes and the public service, a similar analysis needs to be done of all State expenditure. As a country, are we making the most of the potential virtuous cycles that can be generated from its expenditure? For example, South Africa is regarded as having a particularly pronounced welfare system, providing a higher degree of income support than comparable developing countries. Necessitated by the high levels of poverty, this income support is commendable. This is sometimes criticised in a manner of binary opposites: more cash to welfare means less cash for a developmental State. But is that necessarily the case? If South Africa spends R83 billion on social grants each year (many times what the country spends on industrial incentive programmes), how much of that welfare spend comes back to local industry? How much is spent on imported goods and services? To what extent can welfare spend be linked to wage goods, to new production activities in depressed rural areas and other initiatives that build the productive capacity of South Africa? Why do we not proceed to link our social welfare expenditure to goods and services that can be produced by the poor themselves? South Africa does not always get sufficient value from the money it spends, which is what a Developmental State has to do.

All of the above analysis is explicitly State-centric. It looks only at resource mobilisation and institutional issues within the boundaries of State expenditure on the basis that other contributions in this collection will look more intensively at the private sector and other social formations.

However, the focus on the State is more pointed than that – it is based on a view that if the State is indeed the centrepiece to a Developmental State, it is here that we must start to make the most of our institutions and resources. The overriding 'institutional issue' for an aspirant South African Developmental State is that first and foremost it must transform itself into an Effective State.

Discussion

The discussion focused on the role of development finance institutions in a developmental state.

The typical view of development finance institutions has to be expanded in view of their prominence in IPAP 2. How must decisions be made on big issues like new sources of funds for development finance institutions, the value of the rand and local procurement? There is a risk that development finance institutions may get additional funding without either a consensus around their role or coordinated action by the state to ensure the successful use of the funds.

Can South Africa simply adopt the BNDES model from Brazil? BNDES is a state-owned merchant bank. It is the dominant provider of capital in Brazil because it was engineered to counter the risk aversion of private banks. Still, it is also heavily dependent on mining. South Africa may not want to copy this model but it is difficult to get away from supporting resource producers in resource-based economies. This helps to determine how far the IDC can be re-engineered to fund medium-technology industries that are labour-intensive.

South Africa also has a more dynamic and competitive

financial sector than Brazil. In this context, private banks attack the development finance institutions, arguing that they should not be allowed to undercut banks by providing soft loans. The IDC has provided low-interest loan schemes, much like it did in the early 1990s, but the banks lobbied heavily against these schemes on the grounds that they were undercutting the private sector.

The government needs to provide strong support for the development finance institutions to take on a developmental role, with lower interest rates for more desirable projects. Instead, the government has generally argued that the development finance institutions should only fill market gaps and address market failures. That is, they should act solely as a complement to the private sector, rather than helping to carry out a consistent development strategy or leverage change in the behaviour of the private financial institutions.

More generally, the emphasis on short-run profits in the public sector can be very damaging. IDC research shows that the wood value chain is critical in terms of both employment and growth potential. The South African Forestry Company (SAFCOL) is a major state resource in this context but it is now destroying jobs rather than creating them. Because it was instructed to privatise, it had to improve cash flow by increasing the price of logs, which undermined downstream sawmills. The price of logs increased by 145%. Similar problems have emerged around Transnet charges for rail and harbours.

Likewise, the Government Employees Pension Fund is an important source of savings in the economy, with around R1 trillion in funds. Although it was fully funded by the late 2000s, the PIC's excessive investment in shares led to unnecessary losses in the economic downturn. Meanwhile, its shareholder activism focused on narrow BEE that would not benefit the members of the Fund. Again, such issues need to become part of the government discourse.

A particular problem is the inadequate understanding in the broader policy circles of the role of the state-owned enterprises and financial institutions. This, in turn, may lead to inappropriate decisions. In particular, the development finance institutions do not regularly brief Members of Parliament and others who are active in public life. The shareholder departments for the development finance institutions are often overly sensitive about their ability to direct 'their' institutions without interference from the rest of government. This leads to a broader governance issue around making the state sector truly accountable. The secrecy in the governance of state-owned enterprises means that they cannot be held accountable and a consensus position cannot be reached.

We must monitor and improve the processes of policy development, not just policy implementation. It is of no use to ensure the implementation of poor policies and programmes.

Development finance institutions need to consider the following:

- They must be more proactive in the developmental space and originate projects in areas where they have the experience and expertise.
- They have a role in policy implementation. (When implementation fails, it may not necessarily reflect poor implementation capacity; the policy may simply be poor.)
- They must have good developmental conditionalities, in conjunction with a broader strategy. One example would be for the DBSA to have an exit strategy for support to local municipalities, to avoid being permanently based across 283 municipalities. Support could be made conditional on the municipality addressing basic weaknesses.
- The issue about labour-intensive methods in projects is being taken up by the Department of Public Works and its EPWP programme. But the Department is finding it difficult to roll

out these programmes because they require a different way of doing business. Municipal project proposals are developed by consulting engineers, who often do not want to change the project design simply to adhere to EPWP principles.

- Development finance institutions could request mandates from government departments and manage the budgets for particular programmes over a multi-year period. This would allow for effective and efficient planning and implementation. For this arrangement to succeed, a political decision needs to be taken in Parliament and an agreement reached between the shareholder department and the development finance institution.
- Development finance institutions need to be more proactive in the policy space and must do this within the parameters of a well-defined and trusted advisor relationship with government.

References

DBSA. 2009. *Towards a Long-Term Development Path.* Development Planning Division. Johannesburg.

Naidoo, Ravi. 2009. *The Next Revolution: To Get the State Working. The Thinker Magazine. Volume 7/ 2009.* Johannesburg.

12. Social capital

Jeremy Cronin

Why raise 'social capital' when, in this series, we are defining development as the transformation of the economic growth path? It may be because development is also about popular participation and involvement, something that is people-driven and not just a bureaucratic top-down 'delivery'. But there is also a sense of a deepening disconnect between a reservoir of popular energies, aspirations and traditions of the struggle, and what the government is trying to do.

In the ANC parliamentary caucus, someone raised the issue of 'capital' and Finance Minister Pravin Gordhan said that no one uses the term anymore. But interestingly, he did so in the budget speech, except that he was referring not to capital in general but to 'social capital'. He used it in the context of the celebration of the 20th anniversary of the release of Nelson Mandela and the negotiated transition that ensued. He said that we need a common vision of South Africa and, possibly for the first time in a budget speech, that we also need a fundamental transformation of the economic growth path to make it more egalitarian and labour-intensive. He noted that we as South Africans have done amazing things: across the political parties and the racial and class divides, we need to remember what we did in the early 1990s, when we managed to talk to each other across all these divides, developed something of a common vision, and began to implement a new democracy. He urged us to hold onto that *social capital.* Let us reinvigorate it now for the new task, which is to put ourselves onto this different growth path.

As others have said, he did a good job and it was exactly the right tone in a situation of precarious and nervous national and global economies. This appeal to get back to our 'rainbows' – he did not use that word – and our 'win-win' and 'shared values' was necessary. In line with the paradigm he was using, he then gave equal weight to a quotation from COSATU and one from the Chief Executive of Business Leadership South Africa. COSATU says that it is 'essential that we urgently adopt the completely new growth path to transform our economy into one based on a labour-intensive manufacturing industry and one that meets the basic needs of our people'. The Chief Executive of Business Leadership said that, 'South Africa is not making sufficient progress because there is no shared vision that prioritises growth as a national goal… The first step would be for society, led by government, but with business, labour and civil society in close support, to agree on a vision of doubling the size of the economy within a generation.'

There was no talk about what *kind* of growth path but just about 'growth'. This was appropriate for a budget speech and hit the mark in terms of the big challenge. The danger is that we will slip away from it now into disputes of COSATU and the Alliance. We need to hold onto this while we continue to argue about other matters.

There are two fundamental potential dangers in setting up a discussion around 'social capital' in this way. The first is imagining that COSATU and big business are saying the same thing, whereas the class difference is profound and goes profoundly to the heart of the issues.

The second is about the storyline that is being developed in this version of social capital. Pravin Gordhan drew on this storyline: the important negotiation process that we developed.

The danger is that the narrative about who we are, and therefore the social capital that we need to develop, is that we can agree across all our divisions if we just talk to each other. We need reconciliation; this is a critical task. But the negotiated transition and the release of Mandela, as we and the ANC have been saying, were not just the result of a meeting of minds, of some elite pact of two adversaries that somehow came to their senses (although it ran the danger of being that). Instead, it was propelled by a protracted popular, class and national struggle, which developed a whole set of other social capital traditions, of grassroots organisation, popular mobilisation, collective leadership (not always but sometimes), broad movements and alliances. We complain, often justifiably, about this fractious alliance. But the alliance has elements that left-wing movements around the globe, such as in Latin America, do not really understand. We have developed alliances, multi-class strategies and amazing political social capital over a protracted struggle: political education, cadre development and deployment, and traditions of political education, *Umrabulo*, songs, poetry, T-shirts and funerals. And we take the vocabulary for granted: strategy and tactics, motive forces, and the National Democratic Revolution (NDR). This range of things is actually massive social capital, generated and passed on through generations over a protracted period of struggle.

In the negotiations at the Convention for a Democratic South Africa (CODESA), we fought for a two-sided negotiating table: the liberation movement and the incumbent regime. The then-government wanted everyone represented, including Inkatha, Bantustan parties and others, which favoured them. But the ANC completely outwitted the regime in the negotiating process because the regime had a domineering style of leadership. They would caucus in a tiny group (of course, this is what the present government is doing) to determine their line of argument and would then inform their parties of the new line on the morning of some task group meeting. The ANC had the experience of working with difference and building a broad front, and was able to reach all of these other Bantustan parties. There was some opportunism but in the main, a cultural resource had emerged and we completely outfoxed them. That was a kind of social capital. It is not because Afrikaners are different; it showed the value and importance of political social capital.

Social capital is under attack in the liberal media and we often feed it through the contemporary reality of things like cadre development and deployment, and the discourse of the NDR. These are all important but we often vulgarise our social capital; it becomes formalistic. We are not drawing sufficiently on it.

There are two kinds of narrative around social capital. The one is that we are a nation of reconcilers, across all classes and political parties. But there is a different narrative: the narrative of an anti-systemic struggle, a struggle of transformation, liberation, opposition and change – as opposed to 'let us all feel good and work together and find each other in a new rainbow'. Both are necessary. The broad nation-building discourses are important and it is not illegitimate to draw on Mandela as the father of the nation. But there is a huge unease in the ANC around this. 'Why do opposition parties think they own Mandela? He is ANC!' It is good that Mandela is 'owned' by the broadest range of South Africans and the global community. Let us remember what kind of vision we are trying to develop. We are trying to develop a vision that is against the system and the structure of the growth path; we need to bring big capital into it as best we can. We need to appeal to them in this broad way. At the same time, however, we are not going to drive them into a vision of transformation unless there is popular energy of an anti-systemic kind. We have significant social capital in that direction but it has been vulgarised and undermined in a variety of ways.

Basically, there is an elite hegemony and a popular hegemony. The elite hegemony, which has prevailed over these last 15 or 17 years, is the discourse of growth: growth will solve all of our problems. The expanded accumulation and reproduction of capital will deracialise the economy. They used to say the same when we called for economic sanctions: the way to erode racialism in South Africa is to encourage asset investment because the market itself will erode racial distinctions. That argument has been powerful in the new terrain: it argues that, regardless of the kind and character of growth, 6% growth will resolve our problems. Therefore, let us do the things that are necessary to encourage growth: create an investor-friendly climate and infrastructure that lowers the cost of doing business. That is what the Chief Executive of Business Leadership South Africa is still saying: let us agree on doubling the growth rate, let us have a national consensus on this, and that should be our vision.

The popular hegemony is about an anti-systemic transformation. It is a narrative not of growth but of the primacy of social needs. Propelling ourselves onto a different growth path will require us to revitalise this political 'social capital' of anti-systemic struggle and popular struggle, organisation, mobilisation and aspirations. The next question is how, and why, are we not doing it? Why has it become vulgarised?

The academic David Halpern (2005) says that policymakers like us love the term 'capital'. On the one hand, it has its hard-nosed economic feel but it also has a nice, soft side that restates the importance of the social. It has increasingly come into the global mainstream economic discourse and it marks an important shift away from the crudities of narrow atomistic liberalism. It was Margaret Thatcher who said, famously, that there is no such thing as society; there are just individuals – and they are all on the market, no doubt. I think part of the reason that some mainstream theorists and economists increasingly use the term 'social capital' is the failure of the structural adjustment and other transitional programmes in the 1990s. Joseph Stiglitz is an example. It goes hand in hand with an analysis of Eastern Europe that says you can unleash the market and privatise, but unless there are social institutions and a range of other things that are not narrowly related to the market, you get a perverse set of outcomes. The 'social' has come back into the discourse with the institutional realisation that economics is not 'just the market'.

The author Robert Putnam studies the importance of social cohesion. Societies that grow depend upon a reservoir of institutions, knowledge, habits and other cultural aspects that provide social cohesion. This is a critical pillar for any development. He has looked at the cooperative movement in Italy and the United States. His most recent book, *Bowling alone: The collapse and revival of American community* (Putnam, 2000), bewails the erosion of these mechanisms of cohesive social capital in the United States. He attributes this erosion, not entirely correctly, to things that atomise people, such as the suburbanisation of settlement patterns and people travelling to work in cars. Televisions, cinemas and theatres all erode the cohesive things that require democratic public space. It is quite interesting because those realities also affect us and are partly responsible for the vulgarisation and the lessening of cohesiveness here, including in the townships. He also says that not all social capital is positive and makes a distinction between 'bonding' and 'bridging' social capital. A typical example of bonding social capital (but not the only one) is gangs, which are very socially cohesive but only narrowly, within the gang. The title refers to bowling alleys that once were wonderfully cohesive institutions, multi-class and multi-generation, where people came together in communities. Now people are 'bowling alone'.

Pierre Bourdieu is interested in the way that social capital creates not only social cohesiveness but also inequalities. Social capital is also the capital of the bourgeoisie, such as 'old boy' school networks, the Broederbond, and the typical range of social resources of the dominant classes. So, while social capital should not be romanticised, it is an important reality for society and for its reproduction.

It is important to bring the 'social' back into economic analysis but what about the 'capital' in social capital? This is where I become very uneasy. To call a range of things 'social capital' correctly reminds us of their critical importance in the expanded reproduction of capital – which is how I prefer to describe 'growth'. But the danger is that we subordinate this range of things we call 'social capital' to the whole domain of its usefulness to capitalist growth, instead of seeing such things as sociocultural resources that may or may not be articulated into a transformative struggle to meet social needs. This is not 'exchange' value but 'use' value. But how does one measure social capital to validate the discussion about the services sectors? Is it in terms of its exchange value or its value in meeting social needs? For me, socialism is about getting into that logic – but this is not the place for an abstract discussion.

This social capital – but let us call it 'sociocultural resources' – is an amalgam of different things that can be articulated, disarticulated and rearticulated into a variety of different projects: class projects, analytical projects, social visions or whatever. This is where Marx and Engels went wrong in saying that religion is the opiate of the masses. Clearly, religion has often played that role but it is more complex than that. We know from our own struggle in South Africa or from Latin America and liberation theology that the New Testament can be disarticulated and rearticulated into a completely different political project.

Now this can help us think – in a very grand, generalised way – about what has happened in South Africa over several centuries. The African majority in our country used their social, cultural and productive capacities to put up stiff resistance to colonial occupation and attempted genocide. Colonialism was able to advance, on average, only one kilometre a year throughout the 19th century. This is fairly unique for a colonial settlement in a temperate zone on the scale that we had. Think of America, Australasia, Brazil and Argentina. The original inhabitants remain in the majority in our country. It is a very significant reality, and it is a huge reservoir of social capital.

When industrial capitalism arrived in South Africa in the late 19th century, the indigenous people were still in the majority. Their cultures had been mangled by massive dispossession but they were *still there*, with their language and cultural resources. It is very important to remember this. When we talk about 'social capital' and a 'new growth path', we need to hold on to these things.

The new kind of colonialism in the capitalist era seriously damaged this sociocultural reserve, this social capital. But what it did, smartly, was to rearticulate it into its *own* divide-and-rule project, by exaggerating the differences between ethnic groups and favouring some over others. This sounds typical but, more critically, it was a paradoxical process of destruction and conservation. The indigenous structures and traditions of authority, particularly patriarchal authority, were used as a subordinate element of the state structure of this special kind of colonialism. So, we find 'boss boys' on the mines and traditional leaders supported by a large traditional leadership in the reserve and Bantustan areas.

Mahmood Mamdani nicely describes this as not the 'force of tradition' prevailing, but the 'tradition of force' being used to prevail. A set of coercive mechanisms was disarticulated out of this cultural and social capital and rearticulated to produce a particular growth path. These mechanisms were integral to the particular South African growth path. The preservation of these elements in crisis and distortion still exists: part of the rural problem is the persistence of patriarchy over the control of land,

and the fact that about a third of South African citizens are also subjects of someone else. That remains a major blockage to a different developmental growth path.

Of course, the ANC also used this sociocultural reservoir to rearticulate it into a different project. Initially, it was a modernising project. Pixley Seme said we also have a culture. African people are also civilised and we need to belong in this new, wonderful modern world. That is what Mbeki took up in his African Renaissance project. He endeavoured to articulate it into a modernising growth path but only perpetuated the same path.

But historically, and in time, the ANC's appropriation of these sociocultural resources was to transform them into an anti-systemic, emancipatory liberation struggle, not a project of catch-up or 'we are also civilised here', but to mobilise people to modernise and transform. It was not a backward project either. It used these cultural resources, and we still have them today. *Lekgotlas* and *imbizos*, the songs that we sing, all the apparatus that is so important to cohesion and to empowering the poor, the marginalised and the working class, all of these have a long history and are about the reappropriation and rearticulation of 'social capital' into a project of transformation. Of course, these social resources are not just free-floating ideas, songs and chants; they are embedded in rituals, practices, institutions and localities.

During the 20th century, the reproduction, maintenance and transformation of social capital in South Africa typically happened first in the reserves but with diminishing capacity and resources. This is the main reason why we could not launch a typical Third World guerrilla struggle, not because we did not have rice paddies like Vietnam or a Sierra Maestra like Cuba. There were not enough productive and social capital resources in the reserves to sustain it. In Rhodesia, half of the territory was tribal trust land. In South Africa, it was 13% and scattered.

Then the core localities for social resources and the building of popular power became places of work and townships. There were some others, like bush colleges, prisons and Umkhonto we Sizwe camps in Angola, but the main ones were places of work and townships.

In the townships, a range of things sustains social resources but one could provisionally distinguish three types of structures. First, extended families are hugely important in survival activities. One person might be in formal employment and others will drive a taxi or have a *spaza* shop. There will also be linkages into the rural area. There is a network: sports clubs, schools, churches and faith-based organisations, taxi associations, small business networks, *stokvels* and gangs, for better or for worse. Sometimes the gangs play a progressive role, sometimes in the armed struggle – although they often went off the rails – or as 'Robin Hoods'. All are very important in people's anti-systemic struggles.

On this base of primary institutions and structures on which social capital is built, sustained and transformed, secondary network structures are developed. These include the civic organisations that were somewhat important in the 1950s but became particularly important in the 1980s. On top of them – sometimes undermining them but always having to depend on them – comes the more political project of the United Democratic Front (UDF) and, later, ANC branches.

Where are we now concerning all of this? Many think that there has been a significant disruption between a broadly progressive political project and its organic ties with this range of popular sociocultural resources. That is a problem if one wants to change the growth path, first because the growth path needs *to be about* these energies and resources, but also because it will not happen unless these forces are unleashed. Unless we also deploy these popular resources, we will not achieve a change in the growth path.

Currently, a lot of political and ANC discourse is an ironical and paradoxical lamentation for a golden past. At the time, we were imprisoned, killed and massacred – but somehow it seemed *better*. We better understood our values. We were more organically linked to our mass base because we had to be. *Why are we not like that anymore?* The solution becomes a kind of a moralising discourse. *Comrades, we must be more disciplined, as we used to be!* It is abstract and not connected to changing the growth path; it is not linked into those realities.

Politics has become bureaucratic and narrowly electoralist. There is a very instrumentalist connection. Instead of that organic connection to the issues of people in poor rural areas, we visit churches on the eve of elections and ask them to vote for us. The connection is not just less organic; it is demagogic. It is a kind of populist, 'You are a victim, I am a victim. We are all victims of a conspiracy. Identify yourselves with me, my fellow persecuted, and we all deserve a big break – the next tender or whatever – because we are victims.' This discourse is very strange to the notion of popular protagonists or popular activism. One cannot imagine Chris Hani getting into it.

Why? There is a range of reasons, and it is important to ask if we need to revitalise these social resources.

First, it has to do with a very top-down, bureaucratic approach, which is inevitable when a liberation movement becomes a ruling party. It is the delivery approach to transformation. We will 'deliver' and the people who were communities, trade unions, collectives, *stokvels* and the like become individualised, atomised 'consumers' and 'clients'. You obtain a bureaucratic, market-type relationship with your key popular base. You deliver Reconstruction and Development Programme (RDP) housing to them; you do not involve them in the construction through housing brigades. You know what they want. They want houses and you are going to deliver 3.1 million of them, which we did, amazingly. Of course, half of them need to be knocked down; we do not work with people's expertise and understanding. People are farming in the rural areas. There is a rich but obviously declining tradition. How do we work with those resources and the local know-how? People in the former Transkei are saying, 'Why must we ask Mandela to give us houses? We have been building houses here for 3 000 years. It is not a house we want; we want a road that connects us.' We knew what they wanted. This top-down attitude has undermined collectivity.

A second reason is the *way* in which these things are delivered. Typically, bureaucrats like things such as water meters so that you can make sure that when you *deliver*, they *pay*. Yes, maybe users should pay but what does a water meter do in a township? What holds people together in a township? We do know that. There is a strong tradition of solidarity. If you run out of sugar, you go next door to borrow some. Then it is 'Sure' or, 'Sorry, we're out, but try Mrs So-and-so.' When you turn a community into individual consuming entities with water meters you fragment that solidarity, albeit unintentionally. You try to provide them with free basic water but your bureaucratic interventions undermine the critical social traditions – social capital – of mutual support. We are often thoughtless and do not understand why people resist these things. Well, they are resisting also because they want more free water. But if you run out of water and you go next door, your neighbour wants to lend you water but their meter is also ticking down. We end up undermining both the social resources and the user-pay principle.

On the one side, it is a state problem. It calls itself a 'developmental state' when it has delivered a certain amount of goods and services, rather than following a different version of a development state. On the other side, and related to that, is the massive transformation of our political and social organisations, which again is probably an inevitable result of becoming the ruling party. ANC branches, for example, are now aligned to electoral wards. If you go into Khayelitsha, Orange Farm or KwaZakhele, or into a deep rural area, you realise that an electoral ward is very large, either in numbers, like Khayelitsha, or in geographical spread, like a rural area. In order to go to the conferences that elect people onto lists, which is increasingly what it is about (to come and get tenders), you have to have a branch and you have to have 100 members. What do we get? In a huge place like Khayelitsha, with a potential of 30 000 ANC supporters in a ward, you have a branch with 105 people because there are gatekeepers who want to make sure that the members vote for them. As a result, we get the whole crisis around membership cards. In rural areas, the wards and, therefore, the ANC branches are spread across a number of villages. Maybe one village or town dominates and the others are more marginalised, or maybe it takes people three hours to get to a meeting and they cannot afford to do it.

The structure of the ANC branch is no longer what it used to be. In the 1950s, it would be a branch of *these* three churches, *this* high school or primary school and *that* soccer club. Instead of coming from these social capital networks or social institutions, the branch floats above them and no longer has an organic relationship with them. To become an ANC leader in a branch is no longer about earning your stripes by being a hardworking reverend who looks after the people and who has a developmental approach, or someone who coaches the local sports club. It is about who you know and who you can elbow out of the way.

And then, what are the campaigns that the ANC takes up now? Election campaigns and commemorative issues. Mikhail Gorbachev, in *Perestroika* (1988), said that he realised the extent of the crisis of the Soviet Union and the Communist Party, of which he was still the General Secretary, when he noticed that the year was marked by the calendar: the celebration of the Revolution or the commemoration of this and that day. Increasingly, there is this nostalgia for a past that we re-enact –

we walk again out of Victor Verster Prison. But we are not taking up the issues. As the ANC, for instance, we are not organically linked to the problems of *tik* in the Western Cape or the problems of fishing communities and quotas. We are not engaged with those realities because there is a massive disconnect from these huge social networks.

What underpins that? We need to understand that it is not just about these subjective areas of political organisation and how the state conducts itself. There are also other structural changes to those two principal localities, or nodes, in which this anti-systemic social capital has been sustained and reproduced: the township and the workplace. Those two transformations, which happened after 1994 but were underway before that, have also played a role in undermining and fragmenting the capacity of popular forces.

The first element is class mobility out of the townships. Why would a middle class professional want to live in Khayelitsha? Either people move out or they send their kids to former Model C schools. As many have commented, this undermines social cohesion by removing the middle class skills that are critical in any political organisation. It creates a disjuncture between the poorest of the poor, the most marginalised, and those with some skills, resources and organisational capacity. That mobility needs to be welcomed; it is part of liberation. Nonetheless, it has undermined the social capital and the capacity to organise and reproduce it in many townships. (Soweto is an interesting example as people continue to stay; it has a developmental reality about it.)

In fact, we have intensified the problems, for instance with RDP housing. Historically, townships were conceived under apartheid as dormitory spaces, from which people would commute out to work and commute back to sleep and back out to work again. This creates problems for transport and many other things. The more you build rows of houses, without thinking about creating mixed-use, mixed-income neighbourhoods, the more these problems intensify. The transformation of infrastructure is not just about macro space, like freight rail. It is also about the more micro spaces in rural areas, towns and cities, which have not changed. We have complicated and, in many ways, intensified that terrible divide. Other things, like the HIV/AIDS pandemic, the disruption and dislocation of households, and child-headed households have all been corrosive to social capital and capacity.

What is the result? The social capital of the struggle has not been lost. It continues to appear in *toyi-toyis*, marches, petitions, barricades, and the burning down of public facilities and resources. It has turned inward on the townships. Those energies and passions translate into factionalism inside of the ANC, into informal and formal households fighting against each other. Those were also features in the 1980s but then we were often able to unite people around a common project of political transformation.

Everything about the phrase 'township service delivery' is problematic. Why 'township'? Why are people in the township not raising the question of the politics of water or energy across the city and the country? They are defending their poverty, their crumbs, fighting each other in xenophobic attacks and taxi shootings. This huge inward turn is our political failure. We cannot transform the energies, frustrations and social capital into a political and developmental project that would become a vital force in the transformation of the growth path. This raises issues such as production for social needs, local services and how we could valorise those things in *different* ways. Instead, we are fragmenting them.

The other historically important sites for the reproduction of anti-systemic social capital are the workplace and trade union organisations. The previous solidarity has been massively affected by retrenchments, casualisation and informalisation, and tendencies in the trade union movement towards economism and corporatism. There is a kind of defensive syndicalism in the public sector unions, such as the National Education, Health and Allied Workers' Union (NEHAWU) and the South African Democratic Teachers' Union (SADTU). This is in response to the state turning their members into 'employees', rather than treating them as a critical motive force for the transformation of education and healthcare. In the mid-1990s, they were treated like employees and they responded like employees. Obviously, the battle around wages and conditions is the bread and butter of trade unions but the transformational issues are often lost.

Briefly, what needs to be done? How do we rejuvenate these popular social and cultural resources, in new conditions? This is not the 1980s. But this does not make our history irrelevant, as the liberal media thinks. 'The Alliance? It is an anachronism. Cadre development – what is that? National Democratic Revolution? How old-fashioned.' Absolutely not. Although, yes, these things often become anachronistic by the way we vulgarise them. We need to give much more vigour to the different institutions of participatory democracy. We have had *imbizos*, ward committees, hospital committees and police forums. All these community platforms are important but they are generally weak, for a variety of reasons. One of the most exciting possibilities is what the Minister for Cooperative Governance and Traditional Affairs has mooted: elected ward committees that are not party political but comprised of people elected from the faith community, the small business sector, the sporting sector and perhaps the local trade union, depending on the ward profile, of course. They may well be politicos but let them earn their stripes by actually representing and working for a certain sector. (It is not clear how feasible it will be to finance them.)

There are wonderful – if uneven – examples of popular participatory structures in Brazil. In some cities, for example, active popular participation in local budgeting has played an important anti-systemic role by exposing corruption and undermining political manipulation, the same problems we face. We should reconsider the basic organisation of our political formations. In the ANC, should the branch not be smaller or more localised?

Class mobility out of townships is progress, in many senses, but also creates some perverse outcomes. We need to embrace a different kind of built environment that includes mixed-use and mixed-income areas. Our cities and towns are awful, sprawling and highly stratified. The spatial transformation of human settlements is important: we must create more democratic spaces. Our public transport is designed just to get people from dormitory townships to work and then back again. But a good public transport system – and hopefully bus rapid transit systems will become part of that – is one that both middle-income and poor users *like* to use, because it is good, efficient and safe, and it creates democratic space. Down with more freeways! They are sterile spaces that atomise people into individual cars.

We need to provide resources to local community service structures: small, medium and microenterprises (SMMEs), cooperatives, and the like. The social side of the EPWP gets halfway there, but it is still locked into the 'first economy/second economy' paradigm. People get a 'job opportunity' for 100 days, if they are lucky, and somehow that will give them the skills and the mobility to migrate into the first economy. There are many problems with that paradigm but the main one is that it assumes the first economy is fine, it does not need restructuring, and the growth path is sound. It is only that some people are left behind and they can catch up if we recapitalise some taxis or get them some 100-day work opportunities.

We need to change that completely. Therefore, when we resource these community-based SMMEs, cooperatives and other activities, it is not about promoting them into an otherwise-wonderful first economy. It is about changing the first economy that keeps reproducing this reality. So, how do we resource them to create sustainable livelihoods for people and address social needs? Let us not talk too quickly about exchange values and contributions to growth. These are additional. People do not have dignity. They do not have possibilities of surviving. Development is also critically about that. This 'world-class city' paradigm is dreadful: creating cities for the visitors of 2010 and those who will come after. Suddenly, we look at Johannesburg to figure out how we will manage with 400 000 people coming into the city for three weeks. And we all have to have an international conference centre, Blue IQ, and so forth. We really need to change this paradigm.

There is a huge amount of work to be done and there is a dearth of research. In *Towards a 15-year review*, the Presidency (2008) attempted to look at social capital. It provided some interesting indicators. For instance, there is a high level of membership of political parties. Also, the average black person does not have many friends where he or she lives – fewer than whites, surprisingly. These are only some of the transformations; more research is required.

A significant problem is the way the state interfaces with people and communities. This is a challenge for Brazil as well. The Brazilian literature on popular participatory democracy says the big battle is that bureaucrats of all levels – from ministers and deputy ministers down to the local areas – are surprisingly ill-equipped to engage with people and run participatory processes. You see that in our *imbizos*. We come and inform people, and then they can line up with complaints and we say we will deal with those later. But there is no engagement around what it is that *you* actually want *here*. 'What do you think are the priorities? Is it housing, or is it something else?' Obviously, the community is not a single entity. There will be different views and those need to surface. Part of the answer – and it is not easy – is to build a cadre of state functionaries who understand development.

A concrete example of this is Johannesburg's Rea Vaya bus

rapid transit system. The taxi associations have blocked attempts to roll out the system. While those who stand to benefit are participating, those who also want a slice of the action have been blocking it and threatening strikes. Belatedly, my colleagues and I have said, 'Why are we just in a dialogue between the state and the taxi industry? What about the community? What about Soweto?' We had not thought about that. So, we went to Soweto to ask people if they would like a bus rapid transit system. They said, 'What is a bus rapid transit system?' We discussed it and they had some interesting things to say: this route is wrong, right or whatever. But when we told them what the price would be, they were extremely interested and became allies in the struggle for transformation against the taxis. We had a similar experience in Nelson Mandela Bay.

Part of the blockage was that we were late in remembering our UDF skills, our 'social capital'. We were slow to understand how to engage with communities. You cannot tell a community what to do. You have to come in and say, 'We would like your support. This is what we thought we ought to do, but what do you think?' You run a risk because they might say, 'We don't like it, actually. We think it's the wrong priority.' We in the state do not like that, because we have our performance targets. Now, with the outcomes-based 'new management', we are on an even tighter rein. These things can undermine precisely what we need to do. These are some obvious points but I just wanted to underline them.

We need a discussion around our concepts. I was beginning one in the cabinet *lekgotla* where the debate about the 'social economy' emerged. To distinguish it from what? Some other economy? All economy is social economy but there is something *different*, which we sometimes refer to as the 'informal sector' or the 'SMME and cooperative sector' or the 'second economy'. This calls for a profound reflection, which needs to connect with an interesting new international discussion. *What do we mean by growth?* Even [French President Nicolas] Sarkozy is starting to ask that question, for his own political reasons.

When we measure 'growth', what are we measuring? We measure GDP but what are the things we are measuring and not measuring? This goes back to an old feminist argument about the work of caregiving or social reproduction in families not being included in GDP. 'Unpaid labour', they called it. Is the solution to pay for it? To commoditise these activities and give them an exchange value? Or is it about use value? We still assume that we need to get onto a new growth path. Is growth the right word? Should we not say a 'development path'?

Is compound growth globally sustainable? For China to achieve the living standards of the United States will require five earths. This brings in the ecological debate. As Ben Cousins said about problematising the idea of agriculture in an earlier seminar, we need to problematise some of these other big issues, and that then links to how we valorise things.

References

Gorbachev, MS, 1988. *Perestroika: New thinking for our country and the world.* New York: Harper & Row.

Gordhan, P, 2010. *Budget speech.* www.dfa.gov.za/docs/speeches/2010/gord0217.html

Halpern, D, 2005. *Social Capital.* Cambridge: Polity Press.

Putnam, RD, 2000. *Bowling alone: The collapse and revival of American community.* New York: Simon and Schuster.

Siisiäinen, M, 2000. 'Two Concepts of Social Capital: Bourdieu vs. Putnam'. Paper presented at ISTR Fourth International conference, Dublin. http://www.istr.org/conferences/dublin/workingpapers/siisiainen.pdf

The Presidency. 2008. *Towards a 15-year review.* Pretoria. www.info.gov.za/view/DownloadFileAction?id=89475

Part Four

Elements of a Development Strategy

13. Elements of a development strategy

Neva Makgetla

The four core elements of an effective long-term, sustainable and increasingly equitable development strategy are:

- Government fulfils the core state functions that are required for sustained economic growth: fiscal and monetary strategies, provision of core economic infrastructure (electricity, logistics and water), education, health and security.
- The production structure is diversified to maximise employment creation in the short and medium term while laying the basis for increasingly knowledge-based growth in the long run.
- Equity and social mobility are increased through more equitable education and ownership of assets.
- Social protection is linked to active labour market policies to protect the poor and permit greater economic responsiveness.

Focusing on the proposals here would require changing other activities and priorities of the state, for instance:

1. Shifting the emphasis of industrial policy in the short and medium term to labour-absorbing sectors that are geared largely to domestic and regional demand, while consistently but more gradually encouraging high-tech industries as a long-run requirement

2. Eliminating 'vanity' projects that promise but cannot deliver a qualitative improvement in some area of development
3. Significantly reducing the requirements for narrow BEE while increasing incentives and support for all forms of collective ownership and for SMMEs
4. Ensuring greater alignment across the spheres of the state, and requiring state-owned enterprises and development finance institutions to support broader government strategies and be far more transparent in their management and pricing
5. Reforming the training and education systems to ensure that basic education in poor communities is improved, while taking measures to improve social mobility and legitimacy by ensuring more merit-based access to Model C schools and tertiary education.

Table 13.1 maps out the elements of a development strategy over the short-, medium- and long-term.

Table 13.1: Elements of a development strategy

Element		Immediate (1–2 years)	Medium term (3–7 years)	Long term (7–20 years)
Core government actions required for sustainable growth	Outcomes	• Countercyclical fiscal strategy • Regulation of short-run financial flows to ensure competitive and relatively stable currency • Improvement of infrastructure through build programme and greater investment in maintenance by municipalities	• Maintenance and continual improvement of electricity, logistics and water infrastructure • Bottlenecks in education and skills addressed • Healthcare costs controlled at top end and quality improved at lower end • Reduction in violent crime	• Infrastructure, health, education, regulatory framework and safety and security in top 20% by international benchmarks • Emissions increasingly close to international norms

Element		Immediate (1–2 years)	Medium term (3–7 years)	Long term (7–20 years)
Core government actions required for sustainable growth	Outcomes (cont.)	• More consistent and efficient regulation and pricing of infrastructure	• Increased energy efficiency and reduced emissions from other sources	
	Policy instruments	• Appropriate fiscal policy • Tax on capital flows • Improved financial and technical management of state-owned enterprises in order to secure build programme and minimise its costs • Increased funding for maintenance by metropolitan municipalities and secondary cities • Regulatory assessment system to ensure that economic policies prioritise decent work agendas without imposing unnecessary costs or other priorities • Development of price paths to balance aims of growth and security of supply for electricity, rail, ports and telecommunications	• Identification of future infrastructure needs and need for qualitative improvement (e.g. high-speed trains and undersea cables), as well as ongoing maintenance, growth and alignment • Fundamental reforms in education and skills to meet needs of economy and democracy, especially basic skills and increasing meritocracy • Health sector reform to control private sector costs and improve quality of service in public sector • Strategy on reducing emissions with clear key performance indicators and timeframes • Strategy to manage regional and domestic migration	Continued implementation and monitoring of strategies and investment in infrastructure, health, education, security and emissions reduction

Element		Immediate (1–2 years)	Medium term (3–7 years)	Long term (7–20 years)
Production structure	Outcomes	Employment growth mostly from: • Construction • Services • Tourism • Most exports still from mining value chain	Employment growth increasingly from: • Light manufacturing • Rural development and agricultural value chain • High-end services (health, education, software, etc.) • Exports largely to region, with growth in share of exports from outside mining value chain • Reduced cost of wage goods and improved housing and food security	Economic growth driven by knowledge-based industries, building on existing strengths: • Upstream from mines and construction • Other metals fabrication • Heavy chemicals and pharmaceuticals • Niche agriculture and agro-processing • Increased share of high-tech and dynamic exports • Consistent growth in region
	Policy instruments	• Community Works Programme and EPWP, including significant expansion of Working for Energy programme • Preferential procurement points for local suppliers • Wage subsidy	• Sector strategies geared to labour-absorbing sectors, including 'green' activities and production of wage goods • Qualitative upgrade in procurement capacity of state-owned enterprises and government to give adequate lead times to local producers • Integrated rural development	• Sector strategies that sustain and gradually enhance high-tech industries, focusing on existing strengths

Element		Immediate (1–2 years)	Medium term (3–7 years)	Long term (7–20 years)
Production structure	Policy instruments (cont.)	• Measures to upgrade farmworkers and hawkers (especially to give voice to farmworkers and improve integration of hawkers in value chain)	• Comprehensive regional development strategy to sustain regional markets and stability	• Stronger infrastructure for higher education and research and innovation
More equitable access to assets and human capital	Outcomes	• Provision of housing and infrastructure for the poor • More effective and accountable public ownership • More accountable big business (both public and private) • Support for social mobilisation through Community Works Programme	• More representative higher education, with improvements in historically black universities as undergraduate schools • Qualitative expansion in collective ownership, including employee stock ownership plans, community trusts, worker-controlled retirement funds and cooperatives or social ownership • Regulation or dismantling of state and private monopolies • Significant expansion in smallholder schemes in agriculture and growth in other SMMEs, especially in services and light manufacturing • Improved basic education in schools in poor communities	• Equitable access to education at all levels by race and income level • Collective ownership of a significant share (at least 20%) of assets in formal sector • Share of SMMEs in economy at international norm • More accountable state-owned enterprises and big business

Element		Immediate (1–2 years)	Medium term (3–7 years)	Long term (7–20 years)
More equitable access to assets and human capital	Policy instruments	• Continued implementation of existing housing and infrastructure programmes, with greater emphasis on densification • Strategy to ensure more streamlined, accountable and effective state-owned enterprises and development finance institutions • Changes to Companies Act to strengthen transparency and accountability • Continued strengthening and strategic use of the Competition Commission • Steps to make enrolments in Model C and tertiary education more dependent on merit and less on income	• Redrafted BBBEE strategy to encourage collective ownership and SMMEs • Effective support strategy for cooperatives • Agrarian reform with reorientation of land reform to support the creation of economic opportunity • Targeted upgrading of educators, facilities and texts in poor communities	• Continued measures to support collective ownership • Education to support social mobility, especially through larger and more representative higher education and ongoing improvements in general education, programmes for lifelong learning and skills development
Social protection	Outcomes	• Continued social grants for young, aged and disabled people • Community Works Programme as main support for unemployed adults: target set for number of sites by 2015 (e.g. all communities in poorest quintile)	• Measures to protect especially lower-level workers against shifts in employment structure • Development of social funds to enhance household savings on Singapore model	• Poverty at norm for developed countries (10% or less) • Comprehensive strategy to assist poorest decile of households

Element		Immediate (1–2 years)	Medium term (3–7 years)	Long term (7–20 years)
Social protection	Policy instruments	• Child grant extended to age 18 • All grants to grow at rate of inflation • Community Works Programme extended to target	• Effective systems in place for lifelong learning and training layoffs (review South African Qualifications Authority, SETAs, adult education and placement systems) • Retirement funds reformed and integrated with savings levy for middle- and high-income workers	• Department of Social Development takes responsibility for comprehensive support for the poor

Part Five

Building a Progressive Consensus

14. Building a progressive consensus

Ben Turok

This seminar series began in November 2009 with the title 'Prospects for economic transformation'. The aim was to set out the broad parameters of the structure of the economy and to determine what needs to be done to change that structure in the interests of economic transformation. It was argued that unless that structure was changed, the various socio-economic adjustments being made would not fundamentally change the lives of the majority of our people.

Four seminars were planned, 'The structure of the economy', 'The value chain', 'Potential resources for development' and 'Is a great leap forward possible?' A great deal of discussion went into developing a consensus. This was largely achieved, although several important issues were left for further consideration. Building an agreed position among South African economists about what has to be done, even among likeminded progressives, is difficult. This is partly because the economy is complex and because the political implications of policy decisions are so sensitive. This is why we have yet to establish a national consensus around many major issues. Nevertheless, the seminar showed considerable convergence on key policies.

The difficulty of arriving at agreed positions is illustrated by the plethora of economic policy documents that have emerged over the last two decades, including the Four Scenarios, RDP, Growth,

Employment and Redistribution (GEAR), the Accelerated and Shared Growth Initiative for South Africa (AsgiSA), Inclusive Growth, Growth and Development, Redistributive Growth, Restructured Growth and the New Growth Path. This is indicative of intense debate about economic policy. It also shows that we are not short of policy ideas, although we fall short of agreement.

It is also increasingly apparent that the agenda before government is too large and complex, and there is no visible driving centre. Transforming and restructuring so complex an economy is unlikely to succeed without a strong central agency to provide policy coherence and coordination of implementation. Even the private sector is notable for the absence of an identifiable common purpose.

The final session attempted to bring together the rich ideas presented at the seminars. We agreed on the title 'A developmental growth path', which seems to capture the spirit of the discussion since it includes the key notion of development, the essential ingredient of growth, and the need to move in a new direction. The need for a new agreed direction, or path, is generally accepted. Even among those who remain defensive about the road travelled since 1994, a certain softening can be seen. In a recent comment, Minister of Finance Pravin Gordhan, hopefully reflecting a Treasury view, spoke of a new model to create jobs and eliminate poverty.

The seminars agreed that a developmental growth path should not be conceived in incremental terms but as a qualitative break. Given the rigidities of past performance, this implies economic restructuring. Without restructuring, there can be no significant development.

The transformation of the economy presents a formidable challenge, yet we have no choice but to proceed. The essential point is that the structure of the economy has remained unchanged for a long time. The main beneficiaries are still a small cluster of corporations and individuals with a large element of rent seeking (that is, profits substantially above the normal market returns on investment). The share of profits in the national income climbed from 41% in 1994 to 45% in 2009, with a corresponding drop in the share of remuneration. In 2005/06, the poorest 50% had less than a 5% share in the national income, even allowing for social grants.

The result is growing inequality, severe and persisting unemployment and unacceptable poverty. There is evidence that living conditions for many have improved somewhat because of government provision of social services and welfare grants, summed up in the phrase 'social wage'. Some economists are critical of this phrase and hold that conditions for the poor have deteriorated. Nevertheless, there is substantial agreement across the country that the overall conditions for the poor are unacceptable.

Remarkably, even the most conservative voices agree that the system is not sustainable. It certainly does not reflect what the forces struggling against apartheid had in mind.

The legacy since 1994

The South African economy experienced modest though sustained growth during the post-apartheid period. Growth accelerated between 2003 and 2007 but slowed substantially thereafter as the financial crisis hit. The nature of that growth has been questioned but it is clear that it did not result in a substantial 'trickle-down' effect. Furthermore, the structure of the growth path contained imbalances that inhibited rapid and all-round economic development. Hence, unemployment, inequality and poverty remained disturbingly high.

It is agreed that growth since 1994 has been led in part by consumption by the affluent. The consumption-driven sectors grew at double the rate of the production-driven sectors and created a significant number of jobs. This consumption-driven growth was based on private credit extension, which led to unsustainable levels of household debt. There is, however, some debate about the significance of jobs created in the services sector and what may be expected of this sector in the future.

Consumption-driven growth has stimulated imports, which has led to a growing trade deficit. The deficit has increasingly been financed by short-term portfolio inflows. These inflows, in turn, have prevented the currency adjustment required to bring the current account into balance.

Worse, of the massive growth in private credit extension since 1994, only a small proportion (less than 6% in 2008) went into bricks-and-mortar fixed investment. After the Treasury relaxed exchange controls, high levels of capital flight occurred, especially from mining. This contributed to macroeconomic instability. Having lost access to those surpluses and technological capabilities, local industries contracted and were unable to develop important linkages throughout the economy. It is therefore not surprising that, even at the peak of this consumption-driven growth path, the economy grew slower than the average for medium-income countries and unemployment did not fall below 22,8%. This confirms that unemployment is structural and cannot be overcome without fundamentally different policy choices.

There is a strongly held view that there was excessive zeal in pursuing a narrow version of macroeconomic stability, which focused on financial indicators. This caused instability in other macroeconomic variables.

Since 1994, mining and mineral-related stocks have attracted short-term portfolio inflows on the back of the global commodity boom. Relatively high interest rates fuelled the carry trade, which involves highly speculative gambles on the global financial markets. Volatile short-term capital inflows and outflows are liable to contribute to recurrent financial shocks that destabilise the economy.

There is also evidence of excessive financialisation in the system and rent seeking at the expense of investment in productive assets. These tendencies have a negative effect on the real economy, especially as they are accompanied by high levels of collusion between a relatively small cluster of corporations. Between 1994 and 2008, finance and insurance was the single fastest-growing sector: it more than doubled its share in GDP (from 6% to 13%), without a corresponding increase in private investment and savings rates.

Relatively capital-intensive minerals-energy products dominate the production-driven sectors, with limited diversification. The export basket therefore remains dominated by mining and (electricity-intensive) processing products. Per capita, this growth path is one of the most carbon-intensive in the world. This poses increasing risks to our exports as pressure for eco-protectionism mounts in developed economies.

Finally, monopoly pricing of vital inputs has a negative effect on both productive activities and consumers.

Recommendations

The position generated by this seminar series can be summarised as follows:

(a) A developmental state needs to be constructed, with a strong core institution capable of driving development. The state must be able to harness substantial state and private finance to use as concessional capital for investment. It might then choose to direct this capital to productive sectors in the real economy, recognising that the value chain goes way beyond mineral extraction and the manufacturing industry.

(b) The productive sectors must be incentivised to focus primarily, but not exclusively, on the domestic and regional market, with the added impetus of a strong local procurement policy.

(c) None of this will succeed without a different kind of public service and state-owned enterprises. Existing institutions require major reform, enlarging and reskilling. This also applies to the private sector.

(d) To ensure that the process includes the widest possible participation, social capital, in all its forms, has to be mobilised and capacitated.

(e) Arguably, growth might continue without the above but it would not be truly developmental.

(f) The process should not be undermined by excessive caution in government and rent seeking by the private sector. The financial sector must be subject to close scrutiny and regulation.

Industrial policy

There has been considerable debate about what is meant by 'productive'. One view is that the manufacturing industry has been seriously eroded. Since this sector has significant multipliers, it can be seen as the foundation of wealth creation. Its erosion therefore needs to be remedied urgently. The country needs to overcome its dependence on mineral extraction without losing this source of foreign revenue. It is critical to formulate and properly resource an industrial policy that focuses on sectors with high employment and growth multipliers; this will resuscitate the production sectors and ensure that jobs in the consumption-driven services sectors are more stable and viable.

To stabilise the trade balance, it is also essential to implement appropriately sequenced trade policies that promote the competitive replacement of imports. Such policies would be based on interventions on both the supply and the demand side, with an emphasis on labour-intensive industries and related services. The importance of promoting labour-intensive industries cannot be overemphasised.

Another view is that the manufacturing industry is less

important in the present information age and that the broader services sector can boost employment far more rapidly. Adequate recognition needs to be given to investment in these sectors.

Yet another view is that without capacitating society as a whole, no amount of investment in special areas will create a stable and successful society. However, since the state cannot do everything at the same time, where must it start? And how must the available investment be sequenced?

Review of macroeconomic policy

The analysis leads to the unavoidable conclusion that South Africa needs a major review of its macroeconomic policies, including fiscal and monetary policies. It is clearly insufficient to concentrate on the 'financial fundamentals' without paying equal attention to the real economy and the socio-economic factors, especially employment and decent work.

This is not to reject the view that important macroeconomic variables must be stable, that the budget deficit and inflation must be at reasonable levels, and that external financial shocks are a threat to stability. However, these are not the sole considerations of macroeconomic policy.

The financial sector

The rapid financialisation of the economy is a major concern. New measures should be introduced to reinforce the Consumer Credit Act, including curbing the use of credit cards and the consumption of imported luxury goods.

While there is a broad consensus on the need for a competitive and stable currency, limited progress has been made in identifying possible instruments for currency stability. The accumulation of foreign reserves is an important measure. However, capital controls should also be identified to discourage short-term speculative flows in and out of the economy.

The global financial crisis has caused a substantial rethink of the essentials of neoliberal economic orthodoxy. South Africa can hardly ignore this, since its needs are so much greater.

There is, unfortunately, evidence that the private sector strongly resists investment in the productive sectors, apart from mineral extraction. Private investment in productive activity generally did not increase as much as in comparable countries. Also, some of the major corporations have shifted abroad and capital and capacity continue to leak to other countries. The development finance institutions have not been recapitalised for decades and have therefore adopted conservative investment policies to sustain their capital base. Government needs to be more proactive here.

While there is a persistent refrain about the low level of savings available for investment, the PIC, which depends largely on government pension funds, invests mainly in stocks and shares. There is a proposal for directing a larger portion of these funds into the productive sectors.

The power of asset managers

The state needs a far better understanding of what funds, public and private, are available for investment, how investments are processed, and who decides on investments. It must harness substantial funds for a variety of state institutions and agencies, including concessional capital to expand the economy. It needs an organogram of how funds flow, who takes decisions at what point and why this may be significant. *There is a new recognition of the critical role of asset consultants and investment managers in shaping overall investment in the economy.*

Sasol may be a good example because it is huge, it puts large amounts of money into the local economy, and its decisions (even to shelve projects) have a long-term impact. Hence, the way it makes those decisions is very important.

There needs to be strong linkages between BEE transactions and broader developmental goals, such as increased employment, production and value-adding processes. To date, R500 billion worth of BEE transactions have been done, with a total stock of about R1,2 trillion; however, approximately half of these are no longer technically solvent.

There are strong arguments about the economy becoming more competitive. However, it is important to distinguish between being more competitive in global markets and encouraging competition in the domestic environment.

Local procurement

The state must promote publicly influenced local procurement to enhance the provision of competitively priced inputs in the long run. It must take strong action through the competition law to increase competition in the economy and break existing monopolies. Anti-competitive practices and structures must be dismantled and actions taken to encourage lower prices for goods bought by poor and working class consumers.

Local procurement allows local manufacturing and the related downstream activities to raise employment; this increases demand, which positively affects the trading account. There is a potential for local procurement to lead to higher prices for consumer goods, especially if the policy includes higher tariffs for imported goods. This needs to be weighed against the benefits of job creation: unemployed people prefer jobs to cheap consumer goods. Local procurement also boosts national pride and confidence, which are important elements in building a democratic developmental state.

The public service

There is abundant evidence that the public service and some public institutions are performing well below the desired levels. Many areas operate in a bureaucratic manner and provide shoddy services. The public service needs to introduce more rigorous competence testing and provide support where skills are deficient. Its current commitment to transformation and output seems to be insufficient.

The public service must move towards excellent service delivery. This requires capacity building through a combination of a meritocratic recruitment process and skills upgrading in the context of a strong transformation effort. Skilled personnel from the private sector could be introduced to fill existing gaps. However, the education system must produce far greater numbers of graduates at all levels, especially in science, maths and technology. Since there is an acute shortage of professional skills, serious efforts must be made to fragment professional tasks so that lower-level technicians can perform them. China's earlier policy of barefoot doctors sets an excellent example for developing countries. South Africa also needs to put far more emphasis on proper accountability.

In view of the frequent comments by public representatives on the damage done by corruption in the public service, severe punitive measures must be instituted to combat corruption. The flagrant violation of the requirements of the Public Finance Management Act to disclose tender preferences, business links and other abuses has to be tackled directly.

Regional markets

South Africa failed to prioritise the regional market after 1994 and now efforts to create regional unity are being undermined by the European Partnership Agreements. Greater efforts are required to encourage regional integration.

Social capital

Traditional African societies had enormous social cohesion, with some residual manifestations and loyalties. During the struggle years, political and labour movements and civil society formations built a powerful sense of solidarity, much of which remains intact. However, these attributes are not being mobilised for development despite frequent claims that South Africa is pursuing 'people-centred and people-driven development'. The culture of popular participation in projects needs to be introduced at every level.

Agriculture

Some corporations influence the agricultural system and the food value chain, thus raising consumer prices. How to curb this phenomenon is one of the most serious challenges for government.

What should be done?

A new confidence in the economy is emerging, based on concrete research about its natural resources. South Africa is indeed a resource-rich country – according to Citicorp, the richest in the world. But the country and its people do not benefit proportionally from the use of those resources, and that lies in the realm of public decision-making. As Ha-Joon Chang has admonished, South Africa is far too risk averse and engages in bean counting rather than promoting a new and expansionary vision for the economy and its people. This is worthy of serious discussion.

So, what must be done? With which resources? In what order of priority? And by whom?

Index